Tribu
Charlie

"The Pontypool pack was notorious before that special front row made it into the Welsh team. They had a no-nonsense style of play and were as hard as anything nature can produce. Charlie was anthracite... I knew I wanted Charlie, Graham Price and Bobby Windsor together in our team... Their names might not have been on the scoreboard, but they were the reason that our names and the points were there. We were lifted by their efforts. As a scrum half, few people saw them in action up closer than myself. That's why I know Charlie's worth for that Wales team of the golden age."

**Gareth Edwards: Cardiff,
Wales and British & Irish Lions**

"At one stage Wales was viewed as 'easy meat', without any toughness in the scrum. But the Pontypool Front Row shattered that view. When they came along, every team knew they were in for a tough afternoon. They were brilliant and such an important part of the Welsh team."

**Gerald Davies: Cardiff, Wales, British
& Irish Lions and current Welsh Rugby Union President**

"Simply one of the great characters of Welsh and British rugby."

Max Boyce

"'Legend' is often an overused word in sport, but not in Charlie's case. He was a true legend of our game."

Pete Jeffreys: Chairman, Pontypool RFC

"He and the Pontypool Front Row had a huge impact on Welsh rugby. They were known around the world. They all had different personalities, different skills, but when they worked together, they were simply formidable. That's why they are a legend which endures."

Gareth Davies: Cardiff,
Wales and British & Irish Lions

"He was one of those characters that you had to be around, you needed in the changing room; always made everyone laugh, always made everyone welcome. He was just a funny guy; a great guy to have in your squad."

Jonathan Davies: Llanelli, Cardiff and Wales

"We had our own little motto at scrum time, thought up by Charlie: 'We may go up, we may go down, but we never go back'... It was an incredible period, on and off the pitch. The memories will never leave. Charlie was in a class of his own at loosehead prop."

Graham Price: Pontypool,
Wales and British & Irish Lions

"I'd go fighting tigers with Charlie... I played with some greats: Fran Cotton, 'Mighty Mouse' McLauchlan, Mike Burton. Great, great players. But if I had to have anyone by me, it would have to be Charlie. He would give it all for you – every single time. When Charlie died, I lost my Number One. My Number One. And I mean that in every way, playing wise and as a friend off the field."

Bobby Windsor: Pontypool,
Wales and British & Irish Lions

CHARLIE FAULKNER
THE 1 AND ONLY

with **Greg Lewis**

For Will Davies – GL

First impression: 2023

The publishers wish to acknowledge
the support of the Books Council of Wales.

Cover design: Sion Ilar
Cover image: Shutterstock

All other photos from Charlie Faulkner's personal collection.

ISBN: 978 1 912631 46 9

Published and printed in Wales
on paper from well-maintained forests by
Y Lolfa Cyf., Talybont, Ceredigion SY24 5HE
website www.ylolfa.com
e-mail ylolfa@ylolfa.com
tel 01970 832 304

Contents

"I learnt my trade the hard way: Working in front of a blazing furnace in a steelworks and playing rugby in the rain and mud of a Valleys pitch. It was a tough life. No quarter given. But it's where I learnt the art of the scrummage and the philosophy the Pontypool Front Row lived or died by: 'Never take a step back!'"

CHARLIE FAULKNER

Foreword

ONE OF MY greatest memories of playing for Wales is when Charlie Faulkner crossed over the line in Cardiff to score a try against Ireland.

The reaction told us everything about the way Charlie had become such a central part of the team in that first season. You could feel the thrill that went around the stadium – from the crowd and players. If one of us scored, we'd get a pat on the back and a "Well done, JJ" or "Well done, Gareth" – but when Charlie scored, it meant the world to him, so it meant the world to everybody else too.

I can see the smile on his face to this day!

Charlie had worked hard to get his place in the squad, playing countless matches at some of Wales' toughest clubs, where local rivalries meant you always really knew – and felt, from all the bruises – that you had been in a game. Charlie had earned his stripes. And playing under coach Ray Prosser, he was a master of the scrummage. Charlie knew his business and he brought with it great courage and toughness.

The Pontypool pack was notorious before that special front row made it into the Welsh team. They had a no-nonsense style of play and were as hard as anything nature can produce. Charlie was anthracite.

Talk about Charlie first spread through the International scene in 1974, when his friend and co-conspirator Bobby Windsor joined the Lions. Bobby was an unknown but he immediately made his presence felt off the field with his chat and humour – and most of the stories were about Charlie Faulkner.

Bobby would regale wide-eyed English, Scots and Irish players with tales of the things that he and Charlie had done – on and off the pitch – and he'd have the boys in stitches. But the tales seemed so tall that many of the boys started to wonder if this Charlie Faulkner really existed, or whether he was some kind of mythical creature.

Then in 1974 we played a non-cap game against New Zealand and Charlie was in a Wales jersey for the first time. That match has been forgotten because it was unofficial, although it shouldn't have been: a full New Zealand touring side in front of a packed crowd. Anyway, it was a memorable game for me because on that day the scrum held firm. Charlie and the others worked their socks off to keep the scrum straight.

I knew I wanted Charlie, Graham Price and Bobby Windsor together in our team.

Wales were going through a change. We had struggled in the scrum. So when John Dawes took over in 1975, the Pontypool Front Row became the Wales front row.

As that year's Five Nations kicked off, there were questions as to how the new team would play. Charlie was among a slew of new players who would be starting for their first capped match in Paris against an infamous French team – a hell of a debut for Charlie.

But, because of Charlie and the other new players, we were not only able to rediscover our style in Paris, but also impose our authority over the game.

Those newcomers fitted in perfectly and that Five Nations laid the groundwork for what was to come, as Wales went from strength to strength for the rest of the decade.

And you have to remember, Charlie was playing for Wales at a time when every pack we faced was hard as nails.

There was no easy opposition.

France's front row in 1975, for instance, was Armand Vaquerin, Alain Paco and Jean-Louis Azarete, with giants in the second row like Alain Estève and Jean-Pierre Bastiat in the back row – so a huge, deadly pack. And yet we beat them by our biggest winning margin in Paris in decades.

In England, there were players like Stack Stevens, Peter Wheeler and Fran Cotton – one of the hardest players ever to appear for his country. They were all British & Irish Lions.

Scotland had Ian 'Mighty Mouse' McLauchlan and Sandy Carmichael – a first-class choice for any team. Plus Alastair McHarg, Duncan Madsen, Gordon Brown – they were a hell of a good pack...

Ireland had Ray McLoughlin, one of the technically best players I played against and alongside in the Lions, and Ken Kennedy, another Lion.

Charlie and the boys were never facing dud or even weak opposition.

He helped solidify our front row and gave us a base in the pack from which everything else could flow. By the end of his debut Five Nations, we were a great team.

Charlie brought not only toughness but great humour and spirit, which was especially important in relieving pre-match tensions. He helped cement the camaraderie in that team.

But he never approached anything about rugby with less than 100% commitment. When we had our regular training sessions in Aberavon, with the reserves having to make up the opposition, those poor boys never got off lightly. Even in training there was no quarter given – or asked for. Everything was as tough as it would be on match day.

We'd all experienced the intimidation and threat of the Pontypool pack – and there were some marvellous confrontations between Pontypool and Cardiff when I was playing. I was always glad when Charlie was on my side!

On occasion, if we had a good couple of sessions, John Dawes would turn a blind eye for us to go for a pint – without totally undoing all the good work! Charlie, Graham and Bobby were uncompromising at work and at play too.

I was fortunate to get the Pontypool Front Row promise directly from Charlie. It's a fond memory. It was before a Scotland game.

I was giving him some pre-match patter and said, "Charlie, you alright? You up for this?"

He looked me intently in the face and said, "Gar, I may go up, I may go down, but I won't be going back."

You couldn't look into that face and not realise he absolutely meant it. It gave you the same sense of belief and strength. He could have given me nonsense for ten minutes but he said all he had to say in those few words. I knew I wasn't going to be picking up the ball on the back foot – I was going to be enjoying myself.

It's funny now to look back and think about all the fuss there was about Charlie's age. It had been said the selectors wouldn't consider him because he was too old.

We, in the team, had no idea how old he was when he joined us, and it was a matter of great gossip and speculation.

In fact, in 1975, when we were flying to Japan, we were at the airport in Hong Kong when John Dawes ordered that all the passports had to be collected for airport security.

We all exchanged glances: at last, we thought, we'd get to see Charlie's age.

Everyone huddled around to see what his date of birth was. But when we opened his passport, he'd changed his birth date in the passport – not professionally, he'd just scribbled over it in red ink. Charlie laughed, "I'm too clever for you boys! You're not going to catch me out." We were killing ourselves with laughter.

When it comes to life, you're not too old and you're not too young if you're *good* enough. And that certainly applied to Charlie.

The work of the pack is often overlooked. People recognise their contribution but they don't see it like they do the open play. The skill of people like Charlie is in the huddle in the middle of the field. So people don't always understand the skill involved.

But as backs, we appreciated every effort, every grunt and every ounce of sweat, because it helped *us* play. They gave us the ball on a silver platter. I'd always say, "Thank you, boys – that was brilliant."

Their names might not have been on the scoreboard, but they were the reason that our names and the points were there. We were lifted by their efforts.

As a scrum half, few people saw them in action up closer than myself.

That's why I know Charlie's worth for that Wales team of the golden age. It took Charlie a little while to get in the Wales team, but he did it – and it took him a while to get around to telling his story.

I'm delighted it's being told now.

Sir Gareth Edwards CBE

Preface

TONY FAULKNER – 'Charlie' – died during the process of writing this book. But his family was determined to honour his memory and carry on, to ensure his last written words were read by those who loved the part he played in a golden age of rugby.

I said his 'last words', but Charlie had never written anything about his life or playing career before. It was that fact which had motivated his family over the years to encourage him to write a memoir.

I came to the project by what seemed like an accident, although it was actually an ambush. I was with my friend John Blackborow in Newport, visiting the grave of his esteemed grandfather, Perce – who'd accompanied the renowned explorer Ernest Shackleton to Antarctica. John asked me if I'd like to meet Charlie. Within minutes we were around the corner in Charlie's back garden.

"Charlie's thinking of writing a book," John said. "Will you help him?"

"Well..."

Anyway, Charlie was a disarming character. Charming, humble. I couldn't say no to working with him.

I knew he had a great story but what first intrigued me most was how this gentle, smiling, obviously caring man could be the same man who ripped and roughed up opponents, who was a byword for toughness and, well, brutality on the pitch. That duality would be fascinating to explore. And I knew it intrigued his wife, Jill, as well, because even though she'd been at his side for more than half a century, she couldn't quite understand the Jekyll/Hyde relationship between Tony

– the husband, father and grandfather, much beloved by his family and friends – and Charlie, one of the most notorious hard men of a golden age of rugby.

Charlie's many friends had been eager to help him with his memoir, and that support only increased after his death in February 2023. We give our thanks to them all, and to Gareth Edwards for writing the marvellous foreword, as we invite you to take a last walk down memory lane with Anthony George Faulkner, a legend of the game.

Charlie.

The 1 and Only.

Greg Lewis

Introduction

IT'S THE FIRST match of the 1975 Five Nations. It's Paris. The Parc des Princes.

Nine changes. Six new caps, and I'm one of them. We're untested – green. And, guess what, they're already saying I'm too old! Too old, be buggered – I'll show 'em.

The crowd's making one hell of a noise. There's a lot of red but a mass of French red, white and blue as well. But it's just a background buzz, because my mind is on only what I have to do.

I've taken enough hammerings not to let that worry me. I've played in front of the bellowing crowds, against fists and kicks and scratches. On pitches that give way to a sludge of mud when you try to plant your feet. Paris isn't going to faze me. Anyway, I'm not alone. At my side are Graham Price and Bobby Windsor. The Pontypool Front Row has become the Wales front row.

Facing us down are Vaquerin, Paco and Azarete... and ruling the French scrum, Alain Estève: the Beast of Beziers, a brutal bearded giant. Not a bad fella off the pitch, but on it... well, that look in his eyes says he'll pretty much kill you if he gets the chance.

That's why Bobby reckons he'll fix him for us first. The two packs groan and struggle and Bobby's boot goes through, wallop, and lays out Estève. As the scrum struggles angrily apart, the Frenchman's flat out on the grass.

Nice one, Bobby.

Then it happens...

Estève looks up, blood shining red among the ragged hair of that wild-man beard, and... he gives us a wink. Yeah, that's right, a bloody wink. Game on.

And what a game it was. It's the game that set the tone for my Welsh career and for that golden age of Welsh rugby which was to flourish and become world-renowned during the second half of the 1970s.

It's a hell of a story. Take hold, plant your feet – and I'll tell it to you.

Tony 'Charlie' Faulkner
September 2022

Chapter One

The farmer's horse

I'VE GOT A school report at home. It says: "Must try harder at all subjects – but loves rugby." Well, they got that right. From the moment I picked up a rugby ball at the age of 11, I loved the sport. I loved the training. I loved doing PT at school, knowing that at the end of the lesson we'd be having a game of rugby.

I was born in 1941 in Adeline Street, in the Pill area of Newport. I was joined three years later by my brother Clive and then three years on again by Roger. Of course, the year of my birth became a matter of discussion back during my career for Wales. *Just how old is he? Has his time passed?* That's what they were saying before I got picked to become part of one of the greatest rugby XVs ever to play the sport. My age when I first pulled on the red jersey isn't a secret any more, but there's still a lot to say. I'll come to all that later...

In Adeline Street we were living with my mother's family, the Murphys, who were lovely – but we were a growing family and needed space. By the time my brother Roger was born, we'd moved to Nash Road in Lliswerry and a new American-style prefab of the kind that was being built at the end of the war. They were only meant to be temporary homes, something to house a post-war family for five years, but we were to stay for twenty. My mother, Ivy, was thrilled with the new prefab because it had a fridge. A modern wonder! We loved the house. It had three bedrooms and plenty of space – and there was a park and lots of countryside all around. It was because of this open countryside that I got my nickname, Charlie.

I was born Anthony George Faulkner and the rugby team sheets always listed me as A G, but at about the age of 10 my mates started calling me Charlie. It was strange how it happened. There was a farm nearby – Jack Robinson's farm in Nash – and one of the animals there was a big old shire horse called Charlie. I would go up and ride him. He was a fine old animal and it was great fun. Me and the horse became such good mates that somehow my friends started calling me Charlie too. And that's how I've become known to a few generations of rugby fans.

My father, George, wasn't around a lot when I was young as he went off and joined the army soon after the war ended, and was posted to Germany as part of the army of occupation. Me and my two brothers were brought up by my mother alone, and she was brilliant. It was a hard life, but no harder than for the other people living around us. Mum had to look after us and try to scratch a living.

I didn't really see too much of my father until I was in secondary school, when he came home. He had been taught a trade in the army, and so got a job as a plumber for the Water Board. To be honest, my father and I weren't particularly close. I would never run him down but that's the way it was. His brother, Ivor, had become a little bit like a surrogate father in my real dad's absence. He was amazing to me, and very supportive of my rugby career later. He followed Pontypool everywhere.

Newport is a port on the south Wales coast at the foot of the valleys of coal – the black gold which transformed Cardiff and Newport into major hubs, sending ships around the world. Heavy industry drew in people from across the globe, especially the Irish, like my own ancestors. Both my parents were of Irish stock, descending from migrants who had come to Newport to build the docks.

My first school was Holy Family in Emlyn Street and I was happy there. It was a bit of curiosity, that school, because it had a playground on the roof – a fully tarmacked one. It was all hemmed in and safe, so there were no accidents. No one fell off. From there I went to St Mary's and then on to the large Catholic secondary school, Father Hills.

It was while I was at Father Hills that I discovered rugby. One of the teachers was Duke Whelan, who played second row for Newport. He was the school's rugby coach and he really inspired me. It was Duke who really got me started in rugby.

I wasn't particularly big but I was strong, and I remember my first game was at Tredegar Park in Newport against another school. I was 11 and already hooked. I played back row for a while until they decided I should be a prop.

There were other sports too. I played football for the school – up front, trying to poach a goal – and baseball, too. At the time, baseball was big in all the ports, including Newport and Cardiff. I was a decent fielder and an okay bat – if I could give it a clout, I would. But I wasn't quite good enough, and rugby was the thing. I loved the training as much as the games. If I scored, it was a bonus, but it didn't matter to me either way.

The docks were declining when I was a kid but Newport had become famous for its steel. The industry began to develop in the late 1800s, with whole housing estates being built for workers. The towns around – such as Cwmbran and Risca – grew too, with workers and their families moving in. I left school at 16 and went to work for Whitehead's. Whitehead's Iron and Steel Company had been founded sometime very early in the twentieth century and had opened its first Newport steel mill in 1920. It then became part of the nationalised Iron and Steel Corporation after the war. It covered acres of land in Pillgwenlly at the top end of Newport's docks. The plant was so big it was like a town in itself, I suppose. It had a social club, and fantastic rugby and football pitches in Bassaleg. Getting a job at Whitehead's was a pretty big deal in those days. It was the plum spot for anyone in the town who wasn't going to university. The pay was good – upwards of £5 a week – and there was a bonus every Christmas. It was not only a good job, but a job for life. They liked boys who came from families with military connections, so maybe my father's army service helped swing it for me.

As I was 16, I was just old enough to be allowed to work in the rolling mill. The white-hot steel comes out of a furnace and goes down a pipe and through rollers. A loose guide controls the bar of steel as it's going into the rollers. At each stage there is a catcher, who uses tongs and lifts the steel from one place to the next. As it's moving along, it's cooling and breaking down, and it's being shaped as it goes through the rollers. The steel was called 'high bond', which is a reinforced steel for the construction industry. I started as a loose guide for three months and then I went on the cooling bed, where we used to have to straighten up the steel, because sometimes it would get caught. If you fell through the bed, you'd get burnt. Because the cooling bed was dangerous, they'd pay you well for doing the job no matter how old you were, so you could be 18 and have a man's wages. I spent most of my time on the cooling bed or as a catcher.

We were given all the kit: protective clothing and steel protectors on the end of our boots, and catchers had tongs to pick up the steel. You had to be careful. It was hard work, dangerous, with smoke billowing all around you. You would regularly burn yourself. On the cooling bed, the steel would be going at a rate of knots. You'd cut it and let it cool. It was sweltering in the summer. I worked there for 19 years, but I would never do it again.

I was on a night out with my non-rugby mates when I met a girl called Jill in the Westgate Hotel in Cardiff. She was a Cwmbran girl, and we got chatting and I asked her to come out with me. We courted for a year or so, and then were married in July 1968, with the reception in the Glanmor Hotel in Newport. It was a great do. Plenty of rugby people and all the Whitehead's boys were there. Jill and I have been together ever since, having three children along the way: Jayne, Jason and Laura.

*

Working at the mill in Whitehead's was good for the muscles. It was a hard, heavy slog. But I had energy to burn back in the 1960s and as well as working long shifts, I couldn't get enough of a new pastime – judo.

I got really into it just about the time I left school. I joined Newport Docks judo club on Kingsway and met a guy called Ramsey Carter, a docker, who guided me. In the end there were five of us who worked hard, trained and all got our black belts together. I loved the discipline and the physical contact, the rough and tumble. In judo, you make one mistake and you are in the air and then down on your back in a second. So it's not just physical, it's about concentration, and that was important to me. I worked my way up to the Welsh heavyweight championship of 1968 and, on the night, things went my way and I took the title. It was an honour. My first big honour and it meant a lot. But of course, over the years, as I played higher standards of rugby, I had to make a decision: carry on with judo or concentrate fully on rugby. It was possible to have niggles and bumps and carry on playing rugby, but you couldn't do that with judo. You couldn't afford any aches and pains. If you couldn't bend, you'd had it. So I ditched the judo and focussed completely on rugby.

Whitehead's had a team and that's where things really got going for me. They played what was known as junior rugby every Saturday and were led by Johnny Whitfield, who was a fine coach. Very knowledgeable and a good influence – you always listened to what he said. And, of course, it was there that I first teamed up with Bobby Windsor, a tough and talented player who'd been a star of Newport Schools. Bobby talked himself into a job at Whitehead's before he was 16 by lying about his age and I think we'd seen the note going around about trials for the team at the same time. We played for the seconds first and then made our way into the first team. It was the beginnings of the 'front row'.

I enjoyed playing at Whitehead's with some really decent players – such as Freddie Ford, Alan Perry, and my good friend Paddy Burke – and we even won the Steelworks Cup, playing against other sites like Ebbw Vale and Panteg. There were a few trips too. Bobby tells me our first trip was to London and he says we all descended on the market at Petticoat Lane, where I bought a big pair of leather boots with a toecap as hard as metal. I can't remember it myself.

After getting noticed in the Whitehead's team, I had a pretty good break.

George Thomas worked at Whitehead's and he was going to be captaining Newport Saracens for the new season. He wanted me to join him. So I had a trial and fitted in. The Sarries were described as second-class, a step up from junior rugby at Whitehead's. It was a pretty big move for me at the time and I was very proud when I first put on my Sarries red blazer. They played at Sandy Lane, Newport, just by the lighthouse road. It's a housing estate now. George was a good player – a disciplinarian and a very fine man. He's still a friend and remembers us arriving at the Sarries:

Charlie would do a job for you, no matter what. If I told him to sort this prop out, he'd sort him out. Not punching or kicking, but rugby-wise. Stop him from playing.

Chapter Two

"Hey, you boys, are you tired of living?"

THESE WERE THE days when you played for nothing but pride – no matter what your level – and had to keep on working.

Although I'd moved to the Sarries, I carried on working at Whitehead's, of course. I'd work all day, train two evenings a week and play a match on a Saturday. Sometimes I'd even go to work on a Saturday morning before a game, though not catching. The mill was shut down on Saturdays. Instead, we'd be cleaning up round the rollers and getting all the scale out – the broken-down steel that was washed down there – cleaning it all out, ready for the shift on Monday. Sometimes we worked Sundays too. I felt young, strong and tough too.

With the Sarries we played across south Wales, taking on the second teams at Ebbw Vale, Pontypool, Abertillery, Risca, Tredegar, Maesteg, Brynmawr, Llantwit Major, Tonyrefail, Aberavon Quins, Porthcawl, Tenby and Haverfordwest. There were no leagues then and we went all over. Lots of the boys were reps and had cars. The rest of us took lifts.

Today the players go to academies, don't they? Well, that was my academy: playing these sides all over the Valleys, learning my trade, getting into brutal battles all over the place. It was learning the hard way, but you learned everything. The tricks. How to survive. How to improve. How to dodge. How to recover. How to cope with defeat... And more defeat! With every battering, we learned something. I enjoyed going to every clubhouse, too, and seeing the trophy cabinets and the photographs and jerseys of Welsh Internationals.

The pitch at the Sarries was saturated underneath with coal, which came down from the Valleys on the River Ebbw. We had a big tin bath in the changing room and that water was black when we came out of there. Even after a couple of baths you were still covered.

We had some decent players there: George Thomas, of course; Mike Goldsworthy, a great kicker; and Gerry Drewett at centre. Bobby Windsor joined us too. In the scrum, I was one side of Bobby and his brother-in-law, Bryn Allen, was the other. We developed into a pretty good team. That first season we played 38 games and lost just two. Both against Pontypool United. Without those defeats, we'd have won the championship that year. That's where I say, "Poor old Johnsey!" You see, Albert Johnsey was full back for the Sarries. Damn good kicker too. Didn't miss much. In that first game against Pontypool United that year, they had beaten us well and truly up there but in the home tie we were winning, until poor Albert missed two penalties in front of the post and cost us the game. He went around to George's house the next day to apologise. It was a Sunday morning and when he knocked, George opened the door. Albert said, "I've come to apologise, George, for missing them two penalties," and all George did was just shut the door quietly. He was so disappointed.

Oh, Albert suffered for that. We'd been contenders, you see. Pontypool United were champions, but we would have been if we'd beaten them. The following game Albert kicked two from the halfway line!

George Thomas remembers:

I was always proud of the team we had to put out – in every position. At one time we had four sides down there. We used to have a very good following, same as they have now.

Charlie was always one of the quiet ones in the changing room. All he thought about was his game. I didn't have to say anything to him. He knew what he had to do. He was dedicated. It was the best group I played with – the most dedicated players ever: Charlie, Bobby, Bryn Allen. They'd always do a job for you.

I'd played about 70 games for the Sarries over about two and half years, won the Ben Francis Cup and the Monmouthshire League, and had a pretty good time. I even got named the club's player of the season. Jill hadn't been into rugby at all when we first met, but during my time with the Sarries she really started to enjoy it. The Sarries club, which was in an old pub in Pill, became an important part of our social life. Jill and the other wives would join us there every Saturday night and later we would head out for a Chinese meal. Jill watched me improve over my time with the Sarries, and it was she who encouraged me to continue to work hard and really start thinking about moving up again.

And then Cross Keys contacted the Sarries and asked if they could take Bobby and me on loan. This was a massive step for us. Cross Keys were a first-class club, regular opponents of Swansea, Cardiff, Newport and Llanelli – Welsh rugby royalty, packed with Internationals. You had to turn up for a game in a white shirt and blazer! George Thomas told me to go, because he thought I was good enough to go first class.

The game Cross Keys wanted us for was at Taunton on Boxing Day. The pace of the game was certainly a step up. But Bobby and I dealt with it well and were quickly asked if we'd make our temporary loan more permanent and stay on until the end of the season.

Playing for the first team at Cross Keys, we faced not only south Wales teams, but Rugby, Royal London Hospital, Oxford, Plymouth Albion, Metropolitan Police, Preston Grasshoppers and Weston-super-Mare. We also played in the Snelling Sevens in the Cardiff Arms Park, a hugely popular day of knockout rugby which attracted big crowds but died out in the 1990s. We weren't one of the top teams but we developed quickly. Our coach was Bill Camry, who was also a swimming coach for Wales.

We played every Wednesday and Saturday and, although it wasn't the glamour of the red jersey to come, I played with the same intensity and interest on a rainy night in Maesteg as I would at the Parc des Princes – well, almost.

I was to play about 100 games for Cross Keys and I learned a lot. I got to play against some of the very top players, such as Mervyn Davies and Trefor Evans – although often clubs kept their best players back for the more crucial top-of-the-league games, so we didn't always get to pit our wits and strength against them.

I always made a point of going up to the opposing props in the bar afterwards to get their thoughts on how I'd played, what I'd done right, what I'd done wrong. In that way I got a feel for how to do better next time – what they saw as my weaknesses. They'd all be happy to chat and to help an opponent, even the ones who were real dirty beggars on the pitch. People like Walter Williams of Neath, and Denzil Williams of Ebbw Vale. Walter was dirty as hell but he'd always have a chat after, talk about the game, answer my questions. He was knocking on the door of the Welsh side then, I think, and he got a couple of caps later. I was always quite intent on getting better. I was always trying to improve myself.

I had Bobby by my side, of course. Bobby and I both worked together at Whitehead's and played together. We were never big drinkers, as such – not the way they tried to make us out to be. But we'd go out, and we could handle our drink. We were hard-working, burning up all that energy in the mill – well, you could have a hangover and sweat it out. Bobby and I sort of grew up together as players. We were at Whitehead's doing similar jobs and we started off our rugby careers together. Bobby was very outgoing and different to me in lots of ways, but our principles were the same. He'd always be joking and making himself heard. If we were interviewed, you couldn't stop him from talking. He was a great player, mind – he was world class.

Those games at Cross Keys could get a bit physical, there's no doubt about that. Some teams would cry off against us: front rows unavailable for fixtures. It became quite a thing. I remember Bobby and me playing against Swansea and a second row leaned across the line-out to Bobby and me, and said, "Hey, you boys, are you tired of living?" He'd laid down a challenge, tried to intimidate us. Next thing, he was going off on a stretcher. Bobby had had a word – put his boot right through the scrum. Some people shouldn't make threats when they're only going to provoke. That's the moral of that story. (Although I think Bobby also got sent off for that one, so maybe there's another lesson there!)

As for me, I don't think I was violent – that's not the way I see it. I was ruthless. I think Graham Price would later say I was the most ruthless player he'd played with or against. So, what's the difference between violent and ruthless? To tell the truth, not a lot! But I went out there to win – not to hurt anyone. And I wanted to win at all costs.

Cross Keys was a good group of players. We'd always have a good win every five or six games – someone a bit better than us that we'd give an upset to. I played with Jeff Squire there, and a few other good players, but they weren't our regulars. And that was the problem: we didn't have a squad to help us become consistent. We were an unfashionable club, a real Valleys club – a bit proud, a bit 'us against them all', but with a first-class fixture list. It was a great experience, but when you're constantly missing players and short of numbers, you can't really get consistency.

We'd have to pick up players from Newbridge or whatever on a wet, windy night, because we were travelling to a match with only half a side. That's when they used to pay them. We'd basically buy players for a game. All done on the quiet. They'd say, "We're giving him £10 for his petrol." I know Bobby mentioned in his book that we were paid for Cross Keys games, but I never got paid. Bobby said he was paid a fiver and I was paid three pound fifty, but I don't know where he had that from. He might have got paid on the quiet, I don't know, but if he did, he never told me! Only those players we had to buy in got paid, as far as I knew. There were no perks for me, only expenses and some free beer. We'd have drinks lined up for us after the Wednesday and Saturday games. But I never drank the night before a game. The drinking was very much linked in with the rugby itself, the bar being the natural place to recharge, celebrate, drown sorrows and chat about the match.

I'd go to Wales games as a spectator pretty regularly. I travelled to Lansdowne Road in March 1966. I still have my one-shilling programme at home, with its adverts for Yardley shaving cream ('Yardley does something for a man'), cigarettes ('Plain smokers like you like Carrolls') and Double Diamond ('The beer the men drink'). Our props that day were John Lloyd and Denzil Williams – another steelworker. It's quite a thing to see the array of jobs the boys had back in the day. Schoolmaster, colliery worker, draughtsman, carpenter, factory worker, car salesman! The whole back cover of the programme was taken up with an advert for Irish Steel. We lost that day (9-6) but won all the others, including England at Twickenham, and were champions. In 1971, I went to Murrayfield. We won by a point there and achieved our first Grand Slam since 1952 later with a victory in Paris.

As I learned my craft, I began to take a closer look at the props that Wales had. I started to say to myself, "I'm fucking better than him!" They couldn't scrummage.

I was working hard. Just needed a bit of finesse. That's when Ray Prosser and Pontypool came calling.

Chapter Three

"Not me, ref!"

It was in a game against Bedford in my first season for Pontypool that I felt like I was truly becoming a player to be reckoned with – and that I was completely at home in the Ponty pack.

I planted my feet and put one of their props out of the scrum – pushing him up and over the second row. It was a pure moment for me: energy, strength and determination coming together to announce that I was in charge.

Noel Williams, who was coming to the end of his time in the back row at Pontypool then but is still a good friend, remembers watching that scrum from the stands.

What I always thought about Charlie was that he had this power. I played with some good looseheads at Pontypool and I played against a lot of good looseheads, as well, but you didn't see many looseheads who could put tightheads up over the top of the second row. You know, that takes some doing and, after Bedford, of course, I'd see him do it on numerous occasions. In fact, in that Bedford game, they put a back row forward up there and, next scrum, Charlie didn't mess around: bang, up he went *as well*! Charlie was in charge. He liked to be the boss. That day I realised that Pontypool had somebody special. I said to myself: "Wow, that boy can scrummage."

This was October 1972, quite early in my new season. Pontypool had not won at Bedford since 1966 – and that record was pretty indicative of what had happened to our club over those few years.

Back in 1971 Pontypool had ended up bottom of the Merit Table. The following year they were eighth. But now we were chasing a higher prize. The change of fortunes was down to Ray Prosser and the team he was creating – with a philosophy based on dominating forward play.

Pross had been a brilliant captain of Pontypool in the late 1950s, taking them to a championship win during which they lost only four of their forty matches. He took over as coach in 1969 while the club was in the doldrums, and set about honing a fit and hard team which put fear into the hearts of opponents – even if they were bigger than us.

Graham Price had already been there for a couple of years when I joined for the 1972/73 season. He had joined as a teenager, very much under Pross's wing. Then they came calling for me to bolster the scrum further. Graham had been playing loosehead till I arrived but then he switched to tighthead to make room for me. This was the first step to our development as the Pontypool Front Row – we were to wait a while before Bobby Windsor joined us.

I had learned a lot at Cross Keys. I was hard and strong, both physically and mentally, but I was a rough diamond. There was no finesse there – I knew that. What Prosser was to do was to turn me into a real player, and I'll never be able to thank him enough. It wasn't just about learning new skills either, it was about losing the bad habits I had learned at Cross Keys – and kicking bad habits is not easy. Foot position, arm position, body position: I'd picked up all the faults and it's easy to do that when propping – especially when the team around you isn't strong or consistent, and you often feel like you're fighting to survive. All these errors are little things but they add up to put you at a big disadvantage. You need an experienced man to tell you what you're doing wrong and, for me, that was Pross. He knew that if I conquered these faults, I'd be a stronger player. He took my raw potential, if you like, and put the final touches to it and helped me out. That's the work not only of a good guiding coach but of a thinking man, a man with a rugby brain.

He was a tough coach, mind. The pain he would put us through was legendary. And I was a focus of this because for Pross the big emphasis was on scrummaging – something that he had signalled by making flanker Terry Cobner his captain.

Pross would have the scrum out for hours in the rain, practising, practising, practising. After a defeat, we knew we'd be out for longer. On cold nights you could see not only our breath in the air but the steam coming off our backs. All the time Pross would tell us to concentrate, concentrate – "If the other side hasn't got the ball, they can't play!"

Pross was a man with a point to prove. Even as a player, he had been told he would never make it. He had. Then he had come back to coach a lacklustre Pontypool team which few felt had any potential, and he was determined to be a success again. I think I fitted in with his sense of wanting to prove himself. I was 31 when I joined Pontypool and felt I still had a lot to prove and much more to achieve. Like Pross, I wasn't going to accept anyone telling me that I wasn't going to make it. That determination runs through the DNA at Pontypool. There's a book about the club by Nick Bishop and Alun Carter and it's called *The Good, the Bad and the Ugly*. In it, they say the club treats being told it's down and out like a clarion call. I did too. It was on the sloping pitch of Pontypool Park that I would prove myself worthy.

That first season had started with mixed fortunes. With Pricey out injured, we lost at home to Cardiff, but then beat Bridgend at the Brewery Field – despite having Bill Evans sent off. That was a big win, with our scrum really coming out on top. We also had Brian Gregory back in our colours too. In October we went to Bedford, as I said, and beat them, and then completed an early season double over Newport: our first double over my home town for ten years – another indication of the change taking place under Pross. The omens were looking good and the forwards were getting a lot of praise for solid scrummaging and first-rate displays.

There were some dark days in November – back-to-back defeats at London Welsh and Bristol – but in the run-up to Christmas we beat my old mates at Cross Keys twice, then Nuneaton and Pontypridd, and drew 10-10 at Aberavon over New Year. Cob had a tremendous game against the Wizards, leading from the front with some crunching tackles and picking up the ball after a last-ditch drive from us to dart over the line for a late try.

January started with a Welsh Cup win against Kenfig Hill, and then a Merit Table win against South Wales Police – Ron Floyd scoring his first try for us – and a win against Northampton. We then beat a very strong Bridgend team, which featured former Wales captain John Lloyd and veteran prop Brian Jones, who had by then played 500 games for them. But we lost a championship game in London against Saracens, a game which would have put us third in the championship. The game included a 50-yard break by Pricey which sadly didn't quite result in a try.

Coach journeys back after a win would be fun, with stops at various favourite pubs for a pint. Journeys back after a defeat would be miserable.

But every defeat meant we trained and trained. I'd go up from work, after a shift in the steelworks, change and get out on the ground. I don't think I ever grumbled. I loved it. I'd seen what it was like at Cross Keys and this was a stage higher. We were Pontypool and we were in the chase for the championship. We beat Oxford University, Moseley and Glamorgan Wanderers, and early in April we went to Ebbw Vale, where we had not won for six years. This was a massive fixture: a win this time would take us into the lead in the championship, ahead of London Welsh. It was a hell of a game, played in pouring rain.

Ebbw Vale's Laurie Daniel kicked well but there was a funny moment when he took a penalty from 40 yards and missed. The ref blew up and ordered he take it again from ten yards closer. Apparently one of the boys – *not me, ref!* – had shouted something to put him off as he had run up the first time, and the ref, unfortunately, had heard it.

The score was level, 10-10, as we went into the last ten minutes. As we closed in on their try line, Laurie failed to smother a ball under pressure, and I grasped it and crashed in under the posts. Those were big points for us. Richie Pugh converted and we ran out winners. We were top.

But London Welsh were still in it too.

Our season came down to a home game against them – the last match of the season, just after the Easter weekend. The crowd was maybe 15,000 strong and they roared us on. It was an amazing atmosphere. We smashed them 22-3 and that was Pontypool's first championship since 1959, back when Ray Prosser had been on the field playing. "Poola! Poola! Poola!" cried the crowd. I can still hear the chant ringing out now.

Across the season, Neath, Swansea, Cardiff and London Welsh had all held the lead, but we were growing into a real team. Not a team of stars, perhaps, but 15 men who worked hard together and gave it everything. Yes: a real team, in every sense of the word. We were relentless in our drive to go forward. Pontypool had gone from bottom of the table to top in two years. We were a different team now, but the same club – a club with a heart beating for rugby. My first season at Pontypool was a fantastic one, under great leadership from Pross and Cob. I was proud to be a part of it.

And I was embarrassed and chuffed to have the *Western Mail* rugby writer J B G Thomas describe me as "one of the cornerstones" of our success.

*

I could not get enough rugby. I was always honoured to turn out for Gwent and at the end of November 1972 we played New Zealand at Ebbw Vale. Cob was there too. Graham Price missed the game because a Bristol prop had broken his cheekbone. We lost 7-16, not too shabby considering the opposition.

I also played for Monmouthshire, beating Glamorgan at Abertillery in January 1973. Cob was there too, and Phil Waters, Ivor Taylor and Bill Evans. It was a fast-moving game, very enjoyable.

I also put myself forward for the Cwmbran Charitables. That was fun, that was! You couldn't play in Wales on a Sunday but you could in England. Crossing the border meant we'd also get a Sunday beer too! So all the Charitables games were away games. No pay, just raising money for charity, playing more rugby and enjoying a few beers. We even got ourselves a tour of the USA in 1973.

Chapter Four

Lionhead, Bolt and Charlie

WE'D ENJOYED SUCCESS in my first season at Pontypool, but Pross was hungry for more and he kept scouting.

He'd found me and he soon had his eye on Bobby. We'd played Cross Keys and Pross had asked me if I knew their "black-haired bastard of a hooker". I said I worked with him. Pross told me to have a word with him because he wanted Bobby at Pontypool.

Pross could already see what he might be able to do to polish all three of us up into a winning partnership, just as he had begun to mould Graham and me into better players individually. Pross brought Bobby in for a trial. Bobby remembers it thus: "At the trial Charlie put eight stitches in my head with his boot. 'Nice to see you again, Bob!'" I couldn't comment. Bobby's memories are always more vivid than mine.

Anyway, Bobby joined Graham and me at Pontypool – and there we were: the Pontypool Front Row.

As players and people, we were all different. Bobby was outgoing, chatty. Graham and I were quieter and didn't say too much in the changing room. Silent assassins, we were. Bobby was bigger than both of us, too – he was one of the first heavy, physical hookers. But all three of us got on well. We weren't chums all the time away from the game, but when the training or the game started, we gelled together. The only downside for Bobby at Pontypool was that there was no fiver a game like he'd had at Cross Keys!

I was still working at Whitehead's, of course, and so was Bobby. Sometimes I had to work as an assistant furnaceman, turning pieces of steel with tongs and working right in front of the furnace. The furnace never got shut down – the company would never do that. They would keep the mill going at all costs. One time I saw that my mate at the furnace had been working so close to the heat that his shirt had been scorched brown. Picture us working there in front of that heat in the summer. Hard to imagine even for me now. We gulped down water to keep ourselves hydrated. We couldn't drink enough.

Of course, you have to remember that every player was working another job as well in those days. You'd have training in the week, plus you might have a floodlit game somewhere like Llanelli on a Wednesday night, and then you'd be back in work on the Thursday morning. It wasn't like today where you would rest your body in between any of it. Pross would not accept any excuse to miss training. It was hard, but it made you mentally tough. And, you know, you can't just give up when things get tough. I've been at rugby training where some blokes would moan and wouldn't put that effort in, but the hardship meant nothing to me. We turned up and we got on with the job. It was difficult, but we got used to it. As Cob said: "We were a team built on a strong work ethic, desire and an ability to get things done – whatever was required." I'd agree with every word of that and my life back then illustrates it.

Pross kept shouting at us, forgetting names very often but always remembering the nicknames he'd given the players. 'Lionhead' for Graham, with his mop of fair hair; 'Bobby the Bolt' for Bobby; and for me... well, he never improved on 'Charlie', so he didn't bother trying. He would bawl us out in front of the others if we'd done anything wrong: that way there were no rumours or gossip about who'd been told off or whose mistake it had been – we all knew where we were. And the fact that he was on you, telling you what you'd done wrong, meant that he felt you were worth his time and effort. Once you understood that, you knew how to take it. He said plenty to me, but all that chimed with my hunger to improve. I think Bobby and I both felt we'd found a home at Pontypool.

To be honest, I think over the years there's been a lot said about how hard we were, but much less about how *fit* we were. I loved to stay fit and that suited Pross. He'd say to me: "Fitness breeds confidence, confidence breeds skill and skill breeds success. So you've got to get yourself fit, fit, fit!" We not only trained hard but Graham and I were also keen on the weights room. I'd go despite also working in the steelworks, which was a workout far harder than any weights. There would also be four or five laps of the pitch, with Pross shouting us on, all ending with a sprint to the finish.

Then it was time for the grotto run. A lot has been said about that grotto over the years. It's part of the Pontypool legend, but for those of you who don't know, I'll explain. On the edge of Pontypool Park is an old stone summer house, built about 240 years ago by one of the super-rich local ironmasters. Its interior was decorated with shells so it became known as the 'shell grotto'. The grotto is on a ridge seven hundred feet up, and it became a central part of Pontypool training for players to have to run up this hill. It's an ordeal you don't forget: struggling quickly up a path through the shale and stones, finding Bobby spread out, exhausted, but not yet at the top, and then spying Pross waiting on the ridge with a barely perceptible nod of approval as your lungs almost burst. He wasn't there to congratulate you but to make sure you got to the top! If you couldn't run to the grotto, Pross wouldn't pick you.

On a hot evening, you gasped for breath and swallowed little flying insects all the way up. In the rain, you gasped for breath and slid in the shale or on the stretch where there's grass, and felt the rain sting your eyes. There is a hell of a view from the top, back over Pontypool and beyond, but you can't enjoy it too much when you're bent double, your lungs hungry for oxygen. I heard Bobby say later that he wouldn't go back up the grotto again even if someone gave him a motorbike to do it on!

Back down in the Park, training would end with more laps and a game of rugby, before we'd head to the bar to be presented with white bread, lumps of cheese and one free pint each.

We also worked hard on our binding, perfecting it and bringing it to bear on the opposition every Wednesday or Saturday. When we'd go down on the hit, I'd go low, knowing my opponent could only go so low. I'd get underneath him, put my head in his ribs and then that's where the bind came in. I'd bind on him – I'd pull him onto me, as if we were one, so he was helping me, really, with my head right on his ribs. And if he was messing about, I'd pull him harder onto me. Every time his side pushed, they pushed his ribs onto my head and that put the fear of God into him. He had the weight of his team behind him and my side pushing into him: so all that weight was pushing on his ribs.

The opposition could see that we were dominating the game from the front row of the scrum. Noel Williams says:

When those three were together, they were fantastic. It was like watching a flight of a plane, you know. Graham would take their loosehead down low and Charlie would put the tighthead up, so you had that lovely position for Bobby to strike for the ball. Marvellous. The scrum never went back when Charlie – when those three – were there.

But even as we got more and more successful, Pross would take us aside after a game and tell us where we could do better.

We expected the opposition pack to take the rough stuff too. If they tried to collapse or turn, we let them know we didn't like that. There were so many dirty things going on in the scrum, out of the ref's view. When the ball was coming in, the opposing hooker would put their hands over your hooker's eyes so he couldn't see. There was a lot of pulling down too: trying to pull down the loosehead, again to stop the hooker from seeing the ball. Sometimes that trick would be met with an uppercut from our second row. No-one could see what was going on in the scrum, could they? They still can't now – even with cameras, you don't see inside the scrum!

But, yes, there were to be brickbats as well as bouquets for the Front Row and Pontypool in the years to come. Accusations of negative and – how should I say – excessive aggression. That came to a head in the following season.

It was to be a tough season. Late on, I broke a bone in my foot and, despite seeing the break in an X-ray, I carried on playing for several weeks because I didn't want to miss out. It was a mistake. The break was painful and eventually I had to have it seen to.

Furthermore, the game against Bedford – the fixture I'd shone in the year before – didn't really go my way. I got sent off, though I was carrying the can for someone else. I didn't moan about it because I knew there were things I'd got away with in the past. It kind of evened things up and I could live with that. Anyway, referees in England were stricter than those in Wales. In Wales, as Graham has said, the whistle would only really go for two things: the hooker going too early or the ball not going in straight from the scrum half. But in away games in England, quite a few Wales players got sent off in that 1973/74 season.

Then in November came that match against London Welsh. London Welsh were a fashionable team, of course, beloved of the showbiz Welshmen like Richard Burton, who sometimes appeared on their home terraces. We were successful but never fashionable like that. We weren't the kind to get back at an opponent over a punch by running round the man and making him small – we would meet a punch with a punch.

Bobby tells a fantastic story about a game in which the ref was being overly hard upon us, picking up on our every misdemeanour while overlooking the opposition's.

Bobby growled at me, "Smack that bastard in the chops!"

The ref heard and ran over, thinking Bobby was encouraging me to punch one of the opposition's players.

"I'm the only bastard on this pitch," the ref said, puffing out his chest and trying to be domineering, I suppose.

"I know," I said (according to Bobby), "and I think you're the bastard he's on about."

Anyway, we headed to Old Deer Park and won easily, 28-9, but they ended up three players down. Afterwards, London Welsh told the press that we'd committed foul play and they didn't want to play us any more. Bobby suggested that it was because we were playing to our strengths: the scrum. We played hard but within the rules. With what was to come for the Pontypool Front Row, in particular, it's interesting that the coach at London Welsh was John Dawes. He might not have liked what he saw that day – especially the score – but he clearly saw something other than aggression and foul play in us, because he was to come calling on us for Wales later.

Club games in Wales, remember, meant everything. Towns which neighboured each other had intense rivalries. There was pride at stake, working class pride, often linked to local industry, some of which was already in decline. Success on the pitch, even just a victory over a local rival on a rainy afternoon, made people feel happy come Monday morning when the work bell rang. Defeat lingered in the heart even longer in the week. It was our job to win – and we were happy to pay the costs for that.

*

To supplement our income, Bobby and I got jobs as bouncers at the Stowaway nightclub in Newport. Our friend John 'Paddy' Burke started there too.

Now that job was one punch-up after another, and it became the source of many of Bobby's most famous stories. I won't go through them all to work out what I do and don't remember. Yes, at one point I ended up locked out in the alleyway, having thrown out an idiot, and I got ganged up on by his mates and took them all on. By the time Bobby and my mates got to me, I was standing there, blood on my dicky bow and shirt and my false teeth in my hands.

The events of the night we celebrated Bobby's call-up to the Lions have become legend. The party ended in the middle of the night, and Bobby and I headed home with our great mate Paddy driving. Just before he dropped me off in Malpas, Paddy clipped a parked car.

We didn't think much of it but it got reported to the police and we ended up at Newport Magistrates' Court. Before we went in, the three of us ran through our version of events: as we were turning into the road, a cat crossed and Paddy swerved and clipped the car. It was too early in the morning to wake anyone, but we'd planned to come back and knock on doors to find the person whose car we'd clipped.

Paddy gave evidence first and ran through the story.

The solicitor spotted a way to trip us up.

"What colour was the cat?"

"Black," Paddy answered.

When I stepped into the court, the solicitor went through the same routine and eventually got to the same question.

"And what colour was the cat?"

"It was grey," I told him.

"Grey? That's interesting," said the solicitor. "Mr Burke said it was a black cat. But you say it was grey. How do you explain that?"

"It was a frosty morning, sir," I said.

I think it was a good answer. Bobby said it was excellent.

Like I said, the story's become a bit of a legend, almost myth, and Bobby loves telling it. But, as Paddy says, "It's absolutely true."

*

Over the seasons we'd build some fabulous memories at Pontypool – and with some great players. John Perkins, Ron Floyd, Jeff Squire, Eddie Butler. Pross guided us brilliantly and Cob was a great captain, a fantastic motivator and someone who thought hard about the game, like Pross did. We were champions in 1974/75 with 34 wins out of 40, and – across all competitions – we scored more than 1,000 points in a season for the first time in our history. Full back Robin Williams scored about half of them. He could regularly kick goals from inside our own half.

Pretty much every observer judged our pack to be the best in the club's history. And recognition that I was becoming a better player brought new opportunities too.

In the autumn of 1974, I played for East Wales against Tonga at the Arms Park, alongside Graham and Cob, and a young Brynmor Williams at scrum half. It was Tonga's first visit to the Northern Hemisphere.

I also turned out for Crawshay's Welsh RFC, which was always both fun and a bit of an honour. Club President was Colonel Sir William Crawshay DSO, who had led raids behind enemy lines in France during the war. We headed off to play Plymouth Albion under floodlights at Beacon Park and Cornwall County at Cambourne; and also had fixtures lined up against Newport, Usk and Carmarthen. For our tour of the south-west of England we put out a pretty good squad, including Welsh caps Phil Llewellyn of Swansea, Ian Hall of Aberavon, and Alec Finlayson of Cardiff, and we won both games easily.

That tour felt like a works outing. The Crawshay players were told the Monday morning train timetable from Carmarthen, with its stops at Llanelli and Swansea (change), Neath, Port Talbot, Bridgend and Cardiff, and then everyone transferred to a coach outside Newport station. We had lunch at Taunton and arrived at Plymouth at about 5 p.m., for the game at 7.15 p.m. After the game, a coach took us to our accommodation at the Regent Hotel in Penzance, for beer and sandwiches. The next day was a rest day but our time was organised: a trip to oyster fisheries and then a boat on the river, lunch at Port Navas Yacht Club in Falmouth, then back to the hotel. Wednesday was game two at Cambourne, and we came home via lunch at the White Hart in Okehampton on Thursday. Yes, like a works trip. We even had a song:

> Now we're off on tour again, boys
> And we know we'll have some fun,
> But before we voice our joy, boys,
> We will see the game is won;
> For we have a reputation
> That must ever more remain
> For no matter who's the winner
> We will always play the game.

There was also another bit I remember:

> Oh, that we were ever staying
> In the captain's Welsh XV

That was pretty important to me – staying in Crawshay's Welsh XV. But by now I also had the International XV in my sights.

For the Wales team, the 1974 Five Nations had been a time of change. Clive Rowlands had announced he would be standing down as coach pretty much before a ball had been kicked, I think, and perhaps that unsettled things. We beat

Scotland in a pretty dour opening game, drew in Ireland and then at home against France, and then lost away to England. Along the way, there was a highlight when our skipper Terry Cobner made his debut and scored the only try in a 6-0 victory over the Scots. Wales were in need of fresh spirit and ideas, on and off the pitch. There was media pressure, including from J B G Thomas of the *Western Mail* – a man whose typewriter could at that time influence selection – for improvement in forward play. That meant opportunities – and I saw one for myself. It was a feeling which grew when I saw Bobby – who had won his first Wales cap against Australia in November 1973 – getting picked to go with the 1974 Lions to South Africa, where, as well as having a fantastic tour, he spent a lot of time telling the boys about me. There were probably a lot of Bobby's very tall stories but, anyway, the Pontypool Front Row were being recognised.

But I was a lot older than Bobby and Graham. Most players back then had packed in rugby altogether by my age, and I knew there was talk that I was simply too old to play for Wales.

I didn't let that affect me. I felt my time was still to come. And, in fact, I got to put on a red jersey before the year was out.

Chapter Five

Property of WRU...
aged – er – 29?

THE ALL BLACKS were touring Ireland to celebrate the Irish Rugby Union's centenary and they also scheduled a game in Wales. I received a call-up.

It was an honour and felt like a culmination of all my hard work, but there was a sting in the tail: it was to be a non-cap game. Now, everyone wants to represent their country in a full International and get a cap for it, especially their first one. But despite New Zealand putting out a full-strength team, this was not to be. A strange and frustrating decision. On top of that, it was decided to play the game on a Wednesday afternoon.

Fortunately, Welsh fans must have phoned in sick in their thousands because we had great support, but the event seemed diminished somehow and that wasn't helped by the result: we failed to take our kicks and went down 12-3.

Bobby and I had played, while Graham was on the bench. But we'd caught the eye. Early on in the game, when Gareth Edwards put the ball in, we'd never moved. And at the post-match dinner Gareth called me over and said, "It's nice to play with a Welsh scrum where I can put the ball in, I can kick it, I can pass it, I can run with it, I can do what I want without the scrum going bloody backwards." I think he'd grown tired of risking having his head kicked off, diving on balls which had been fumbled by our scrum.

Barry Llewelyn had been the tighthead in that game and we had gone back in the scrum on his side, but if they brought Graham in, I knew we'd do for Wales what we did for Pontypool.

Anyway, this was November 1974. I don't know whether Gareth had a word with the selectors – I've always felt he did – but with all eyes on the Five Nations of 1975, we found ourselves getting picked. You see (and I'm not talking about Gareth here), there was a lot of criticism about the Pontypool Front Row then, not just from pundits but players too. But all the backs we celebrate for their skill – like Gareth and Phil Bennett – wanted to play with us, because they all wanted the ball going forward so they weren't caught on the back foot.

What did getting the call-up to the full squad mean to me? Well, as George Thomas, my skipper at Sarries says, I'd dedicated myself to it. For me, back then, it was an honour which is pretty hard to put into words. Emotions which a rugby player can't describe – you need to be a poet. For some players it was more than sport: it was an extension of their nationalism, of their relationship with the country of their birth. It was that for me, I suppose, too – that's only natural – but it was much more about being the best player I could be. Showing that I was worthy of the jersey after all that time. Not getting a cap for that New Zealand game was a disappointment – especially now, looking back, when players get caps as substitutes! I mean we played a full strength All Blacks team with a hell of a scrum and got nothing for it!

But now the Wales Number 1 jersey was mine. I'd be playing for Wales in the Five Nations Championship. And against France at the Parc des Princes!

I was on a high. I nearly scored in the trial and still have a letter from my friend, Lieutenant Colonel David Cox at the Royal Regiment of Wales, sending congratulations from all of the 3rd (Volunteer) Battalion on my "first 'official' cap". I'd been a signaller in the TA for a long time (Bobby too).

I enjoyed the discipline, and it was a good source of extra income. (There was a time when I was working three jobs – teaching judo, the TA and my day job at Whitehead's – plus rugby!) Anyway, the Lieutenant Colonel had seen my trial a few days earlier and said he felt for me when I nearly scored. "Hope you get a similar chance against France!"

Such was my life then – we weren't professional sportsman concentrating on club and country alone. The Lieutenant Colonel asked if I could fit in some more games for the TA, who I'd turned out for before. He hoped I'd be able to play in February, although he realised International calls might get in the way, and get to London for a game that March, which he offered me a lift to. Playing for Wales also meant we couldn't take any overtime shifts at Whitehead's on a Thursday or Sunday, so Bobby and I lost quite a lot of cash. As International players in the 1970s, we were to be a very particular type of celebrity – having fame without the fortune. I mean, every time we did anything on the television and there was a fee involved, we'd get a letter from the WRU saying, "What charity would you like the money to be paid to?" One time later on, Knorr Soups paid Bobby and me £50 to turn up at shops in Cwmbran and Pontypool – you know, make an appearance – and we had a letter telling us to give the money back. What a difference from today! By the way, after taking the Knorr money back off us, the WRU did a deal with Knorr and made the advertising money for itself!

But despite the lack of glamour off the pitch, there was plenty of glamour about being a Wales player on it. And the fact that Graham, Bobby and I would all be playing was a big story, of course. The newspapers even sent a photographer to the mill to take shots of Bobby and me at work. The steel men of Wales!

This Championship was to start with a new team at the top: coach John Dawes took over from Clive Rowlands, and Mervyn Davies took over from Gareth Edwards as captain.

And we were to be a team of new stars, new blood coming in to support the backbone of the 1971 team (Gareth Edwards, JPR, Mervyn Davies and Gerald Davies). This new blood would take Wales to new levels during the second half of the 1970s. There were to be other new caps besides Graham and me: Trefor Evans, John Bevan, Ray Gravell and Steve Fenwick. Despite what John Dawes had said about Pontypool after our game at London Welsh, he was to build the dominance which was to come on us forwards: we were the platform for what would happen in open play and the cause of fear in the opposition. The Pontypool Front Row was to be the Wales front row. A proud moment for us and a proud moment for Pross, who later said he almost cried when he heard we'd all been selected.

I joined the training set-up down at the Aberavon seafront, where we'd change in dorms, run and play on the sand, and get fortified against the wind by tins of soup. Crowds came to watch this spectacle because the 30-man squad were all wearing the hallowed red tracksuit. New coach John Dawes did a lot to improve training and encourage an upgrade in the facilities. He was a thoughtful coach, who considered everything with care. Like Pross, he was a shrewd tactician.

This would be the start of events which would take the Pontypool Front Row to another level – the real start of the legend, I suppose. Playing for Wales made every player a household name, but we were a special unit. Like musketeers. And we were very marketable. I've kept a load of paraphernalia from my rugby career and I've been picking through it as I write this. One cartoon depicted us with our jerseys stamped 'Property of WRU'. Club had become country. The *Daily Mail* featured me under the headline 'Charlie the Ironmonger'. I was the man who went from "black belt to Welsh cap" and was "arriving at [my first] cap... after breaking his nose, fracturing a foot and losing a top row of teeth on the way".

I told Peter Jackson at the *Mail*:

I don't consider rugby a dirty game or that foul play is increasing. It's hard, it's tough, but it's not dirty. I know what I'm talking about because it's hardest of all in the front row.

I've never complained about the knocks because I accept them as part of the game, even down to my front teeth coming out one by one. I get on with the job of playing hard.

That was my philosophy going into my Wales career pretty much summed up in a few sentences.

Although the age against my name... that was 29. Not quite right. The article came out on 15 January, so I was nearly 34. The previous season Delme Thomas had retired from rugby at 31.

In the article, Jackson wrote that I was a fifteen-and-a-half stone prop who had "all the qualities of the indestructible". I was hoping he was right as we prepared to head to Paris.

Chapter Six

Bobby's boot and Merv's cigarette

THAT DEBUT GAME was to be played on January 18, 1975. I've still got all my notes for the trip, so you might be interested to know how those weekends went. The notes we had from the WRU about matches abroad were always headed: "Do you have your passport?"

The meeting point for the team and reserves was the Angel Hotel in Cardiff at 2 p.m. on the Thursday. Then we crossed the road to the training ground at the Arms Park for two hours of training, before going back to the Angel for dinner. Players were then allowed to go to the cinema if they wished. Friday started with breakfast at 8 a.m., and then we boarded the coach at 11.30 and headed for what was then called Glamorgan Airport at Rhoose. The Cambrian Airways plane took off at 12.20, with lunch on board. It was 2.30 p.m. local time when we set down in Orly Airport and got the coach to Hotel Terminus in St Lazare. The evening was dinner at the hotel, with the committee heading to a restaurant for a dinner-jacketed affair. After dinner we all went to the theatre or the cinema. Gerry Lewis, the physio, organised that and he'd keep an eye on us, making sure no-one strayed away from the group and tried to get some beers down them.

Saturday. Match day. The morning was free, with lunch at noon. At 1.15 we took the coach to the Parc des Princes. Shortly before the game, John Dawes took a step back and

Mervyn Davies gave us the speech. I don't think us new boys needed motivation, to be honest: we were playing for Wales – a dream – but any word which would bring us together as a team, galvanise us for that trial to come, was worth listening to. After the game, we had drinks at the hotel and then headed to the Grand Hotel for a dinner. That was our bow ties and dinner jackets event. Sunday was travel home day. The coaches picked us up at 10 a.m. and we were back in Cardiff by early afternoon. The last note in the WRU info for players was a request that we ensure all our personal charges at the hotel in Paris were settled before we checked out.

The game itself? Well, the press didn't give us much of a chance. It was all change in red, as I've said, and they weren't sure. Amidst the hullabaloo of Clive Rowlands announcing during the previous Championship that he was stepping down, we'd also had a pretty lacklustre Five Nations in 1974. Though the press weren't confident, Wales fans saw the changes and were expectant. We always are, aren't we?

In the changing room, I was ready first. This was always the case. I was always raring to go. Ready fifteen minutes before everyone else, prowling around looking for something to do. I savoured every drop of being a player.

Once out there, the Pontypool Front Row went into action from the off. We weren't intimidated by Vaquerin, Paco and Azarete, although they gave us every impression they'd be just as happy to kill us as to win the game, and we went at them for the whole 80 minutes. Estève tried his best, with punches coming through at us from the second row. The cheeky beggar would usually shout Bobby's name before swinging a fist into his face. Eventually, Bobby said to me, "Next scrum, I'll fix him," and, when we went down into the scrum, he booted him in the mouth as hard as he could and then started a brawl.

When everyone separated, Bobby and I looked down at Estève. He was laid out in the mud, his mouth all beard and blood. Then he focussed his eyes on us and gave Bobby a wink. It was going to be a long game.

Bobby says he turned to me and said, "He's given me the wink. What am I going to do now?"

Apparently I replied, "Try kissing him. If that doesn't work, tell him he's wanted on the phone."

Well, now we were in it. Bobby was a wanted man. Every time we bound, one of their props took Bobby's ear in his mouth and held onto it. Imagine the pain of that! If Bobby moved, he was going to get it ripped off. I told him I'd help him out, so I swung an uppercut through and laid the Frenchman out. Unfortunately, his teeth had been clamped around Bobby's lughole when his jaw got cracked. Sixteen stitches Bobby said he had for the tear. None of us went home on a Sunday after a match with that lot looking quite the same as when we left home before the match.

Another massive issue we had that day was the noise in the stadium. It was so loud, with the cheering and the bands, we couldn't hear the line-out signals. So in the end Merv called us together and gestured with his fingers: "One is short, two middle, three long, and the fist is over the top."

So each time we had a line-out, we had this signal. Of course, Gareth was shouting orders as well, just to confuse them. It was a simple thing and yet it worked. A brilliant bit of code.

The strength of our pack that day allowed us to break out and get tries from Steve Fenwick in the opening minutes, then Cob, Gerald Davies, and a cracker from Gareth Edwards in the second half. I think throughout the game Gareth felt pretty freed up by the dominance of the pack – just as he'd hoped.

And then our fifth try – in injury time – went to Graham. The French spilled possession around our 22 and Graham kicked the ball upfield, setting off in pursuit with J J Williams alongside. JJ forced Jean-Pierre Lux to spill the ball and

Graham, still up with the play, grasped it and crossed over for the try. It's amazing to watch the footage now. Not only had Graham kept up with JJ, but I had too. When Graham threw the ball up in the air in excitement after scoring, I was there to catch it! Pricey always mentions in his speeches that the first two forwards up there to congratulate him were me and Bobby. The fact that the three of us were there, after the full 80 minutes, all goes back to what Pross always used to say about the importance of fitness.

And here's another thing: I read later that Graham's try was the first by a Welsh prop in Paris since 1957. The scorer that day? Ray Prosser. Pross is always there somewhere in our story.

Our France game ended 25-10. Victory in Paris! And even the French writers acknowledged that the Pontypool Front Row was a great front row.

It didn't sink in on the pitch, but when we got back in the changing room, we felt such elation. And then that night in the hotel the WRU President Harry Bowcott presented me with my first cap. Later, Alain Estève came looking for Bobby, the man who'd booted him in the mouth... and took him out drinking in the nightclubs of Pigalle.

I came back home to Newport and my wife told me that she hadn't watched the game at all. She'd been out shopping in the market when the game was on and everyone was watching or listening to it. Perhaps Jill was the only one in Wales who wasn't following the game. Wives, generally, were shut out in those days. There were only men at the post-match dinners. At home games, for instance, we'd all be at the Angel Hotel while the women had to go off around Cardiff to find something to eat.

The newspaper columns were filled with our victory but we had to remember it was only the first game – the first game of our new team, the first of the Championship. Next up, we were going to put out an unchanged team against

England, who were captained by Fran Cotton, the Test prop from the Lions' unbeaten tour of South Africa the summer before. Although we were at home, England were favourites and the dressing room before the game was unusually quiet. Even Bobby had no banter in him.

But it wasn't fear. It was concentration, determination. You could feel the tension in the air – it was as if the air was dense with it. It felt as if the walls of the changing room were closing in. I thought to myself, "These buggers are ready to go out and die for the game today." The look in their eyes, their faces. I'd never experienced an atmosphere like that.

Then John Dawes walked in and went to give his talk, but after he looked around the room and saw that everybody was just looking through him, he just nodded at his captain. "Over to you, Merv." Nobody needed to say much, but Merv said a few words and then we were out, unleashed.

All the pre-match talk had been that Fran Cotton was going to cause havoc for us, but he never did. I had the better of him that day. I never had a lot of trouble with Cotton, no. Three tries – from JJ, Fenwick and Gerald – helped us to a 20-4 win, although it wasn't one of our better performances. Although England had never been in the hunt, we had to admit we'd really let them off the hook in the second half – having been 16-0 up at the break. We didn't want to repeat that in later games.

I always liked beating England. It was the 'old enemy'-type thing. In fact, I never lost against them. I won every game I was in against them.

One other thing to say about that game – it's hard to believe it now, but after Merv gave his short pre-match talk in that electric atmosphere in the changing room, he stepped to one side and lit up a cigarette. He drew hard on it for a couple of drags and then, as he turned to go out, he gave it to Gerry Lewis, the physio. Now, Gerry hated smoking. Merv said to Gerry, "Hold this until I get back!" And Gerry was so caught up in the atmosphere that he took the fag, tapped it out and held onto it until the end of the game. When Merv came back into the changing room, Gerry handed him the cigarette and Merv lit it back up!

Different times!

Murrayfield was always a mad atmosphere. I don't know how many turned up to see us that year but they said it was a record crowd for a match in the British Isles. More than 104,000. It was St David's Day – and it should have been our day, but the Scots spoiled it by disrupting our backs and putting Gareth under constant pressure.

The Scots pack were no slouches either, and Ian 'Mighty Mouse' McLauchlan was on blistering form. He'd told his boys to "give Wales hell", and they did. I remember having to drag Graham off Sandy Carmichael at one point. Our woes grew in the first half when we lost John Bevan and Steve Fenwick to injury. Phil Bennett came on as a first-half replacement for Bevan, and didn't have his finest game. Benny came on with the tension high and struggled to get to the pace of the game. He admitted afterwards that he ran when he should have kicked, and kicked when he should have run. It was his worst performance for Wales but they didn't drop him later on, and that was wise because he always served us well after that. In injury time, Trefor Evans crossed over for a try, but Allan Martin missed the conversion from the touchline with the final kick of the match, and we went down 12-10.

I always loved trips to Scotland. The Scottish players always treated us well and with respect – as we did them. The fans always created a wonderful atmosphere, but never hostile. Only Paris really intimidated – with all the noise of the bands and the cockerels running around the place.

That narrow defeat in Edinburgh put the Grand Slam out of our grasp, but the Championship was still wide open. It could be ours or Ireland's, shared, or even Scotland's if we drew and they beat England. All we had to do was recover from the Scottish disappointment and beat Ireland, the previous season's champions. The Irish didn't have a creative side at the time, but they were great spoilers and were deadly at capitalising on errors. They had a tough pack too, with a couple of extremely experienced big names, Willie John McBride and Ray McLoughlin, demanding our respect.

But to be honest, we looked like a different team to the one that took the pitch at Murrayfield. The display we put on against Ireland was one of our best. "Magnificent," JBG called it. "Clever, strong, fast-moving, without the slightest blemish." It was the 80 minutes over which everything John Dawes had been trying to do since he took over the previous September just came together. Poor Phil Bennett, who'd had a mare at Murrayfield, was back on brilliant form. Complete redemption for Benny. We, in the pack, dominated under Merv's leadership. "Expert technicians," JJ called the Pontypool Front Row, "and never less than completely ruthless".

And the fixture brought a particularly special moment for me. I remember it all. Bobby passed me the ball – a fact which he has reminded me of a few times over the years! And I smashed my way over for a try. Mine was the third of five Welsh tries that day. It was a proud moment for me because of my age and all the rest of it, which so many people did remind me of, especially the press. When I read the papers after a game, they wouldn't talk about my performance, they talked about my age. I found that frustrating. It was always 'veteran Faulkner', or words to that effect. They never, ever talked about my performance. That just reinforced a sense in me that I had more to prove than just about anybody else on the pitch.

That's why now when I look in the history books, I love to look up that game. My name on the list of try scorers alongside Gareth Edwards, Gerald Davies, J J Williams and Roy Bergiers.

The 32-4 scoreline was Ireland's heaviest defeat for 68 years. And sadly for the great Willie John McBride, it was his last game in green. Nice guy, Willie John, and a great servant for his country. McLoughlin and Ken Kennedy also bowed out that day.

But, for us, there was nothing but celebration. England beat Scotland, and we were the champions. Merv won the *Rugby Annual for Wales* Player of the Year for the way he led us. With inspiration and determination. Us six new caps got a special mention from the annual too. We "all proved [our] worth in a memorable manner".

Away from Wales and Pooler duties I played and scored for Carwyn James' International XV in Newport's centenary celebrations game, and played a few times for the Barbarians on their Easter 1975 tour around Wales. I almost had a clean sweep of wins for the Baa-Baas but we lost at Cardiff when I had to play as hooker because we were down to 14 men. It was always unfair that replacements weren't allowed in those games, but I was chuffed to play for the Barbarians. They were like the posh side. It got posher when we were invited for a dinner with Prince Charles. He came over to Jill and me and talked to us for about ten minutes. We had our photo taken with him.

In the summer there was a special dinner at Whitehead's Works for Bobby after he led them to the inter-works title. Bobby was honoured with a silver trophy in recognition of his selection to tour South Africa with the British & Irish Lions in 1974. As a former Whitehead's player I received a presentation too – a watch – in recognition of having made my Wales debut that year.

At the end of the season, J B G Thomas chose his top six Welsh players: the players who, in no particular order, had given him "special pleasure as a watcher and critic". Gareth Edwards was there, and Mervyn Davies, Phil Bennett, Allan Martin and Trefor Evans.

The sixth? Well, I was overjoyed to see it was me. It was a kind tribute which made me blush, noting that with Graham and Bobby, I'd formed a "powerful, well-knit, fast-moving and try-scoring front row". I was, he added, an "excellent example of how hard a modern prop should work in the tight and loose".

There was also, of course, the matter of my age. I had, he wrote, "crashed" my way into the national team "after passing the 30 mark" – an "achievement for a forward". Ahem – 30! If he'd known I was 34, I wonder what he would have added?!

It's embarrassing to see some of that in print. But I was proud to be a part of that front row and those teams. I was happy and I was someone who had worked hard and learnt my craft – a dedicated prop.

Chapter Seven

"If you lose, don't come home!"

A COUPLE OF weeks after the 1975 Five Nations, I was told I'd been picked for my first Wales tour – the history-making tour of Japan.

Rugby was a growing sport in Japan. Not only had the national team come to Wales in 1973, they'd also played in England, New Zealand and Australia. The 1973 tour had been an important one for Japan and for WRU President Les Spence, who'd been a prisoner of the Japanese during the Second World War. Having suffered so much in camps in Java and Japan, Les had said that after the war ended, Japan was the last place on earth he would have wanted to visit again. But now he was going back to be treated as an honoured guest. It turned out to be an emotional trip for Les. He'd struck up a friendship with the Japanese manager, Shiggy Konno, who'd been in line to be a kamikaze pilot towards the end of the war, and had been saved from having to fly a suicide mission by the Japanese surrender. Les and Shiggy had been open and honest about their wartime experiences and that's why they'd become friends. "The war will never be forgotten, nor will the friends we lost," Les said. "But we are looking at a new era and whatever I have inwardly will remain there."

We'd all grown up associating Japan with the war and, to be honest, with cruelty to people like Les. My Uncle Trevor had been captured during the surrender of Singapore in 1942 and had been a POW like Les. When Trevor came home, he was really ill – his life was ruined. That was what I thought of the Japanese.

In fact, I spoke to Uncle Trevor before leaving and asked him what he thought of the tour. "Listen," he said, "if you lose, don't come home!" I told the Japanese press this during an interview and it made big headlines!

Les, who was made honorary manager because of his association with Japan, and John Dawes, his assistant, wrote to congratulate me on my inclusion. "We are looking forward to a very happy and successful tour and hope that during the coming summer you will keep reasonably fit."

Japan in 1975 was different: an 'economic powerhouse', they called it. We all had business cards made up. Mine said 'A G Faulkner. Prop. Steelworker.'

Because we were touring in September, it meant training in the heat of August. It isn't always warm in Wales in August but when we met for our first workout at the Police Ground in Bridgend on 13 August, the sun was blazing down.

John Dawes outlined his match plan, telling us we'd go all-out from the start to build a big lead and then try to hold on to it as we tired in the humidity of Japan. That's what we worked on over the following three sessions.

We also got measured for new suits for the tour, and received a visit from some representatives from the Berni Inn chain of restaurants – they had places in Tokyo and were to be our guides to the local food and customs. We were told we'd need regular massages and would need to take tablets to combat dehydration – in fact, physio Gerry Lewis carried 4,000 of those tablets in his bags, as well as new ultrasonic equipment to help with muscle injuries. Us Pontypool boys were pretty well-prepared, having had several summer training sessions. I reckon we were the fittest club in Wales, and Bobby agrees.

Les Spence said he was flying to Japan with not only the best squad in Europe but the best in the world. I think that showed the Japanese a lot of respect – they were undoubtedly a second-class rugby nation at the time, but we took our best squad. I think the professionalism we showed on the tour was to help not only us, but Japan and its development of the game, and maybe even contributed to rugby's growth and Japan's eventual hosting of the World Cup in 2019.

We flew out via Hong Kong, where we beat a Colony XV 57-3, and arrived in Japan to quite a bit of excitement.

The Japanese rugby administrators saw Wales as the top rugby nation, and one willing to help its growth. Back in 1973, manager Shiggy Konno had been glad Wales put out its strongest XV for their touring team because he wanted his players to play the best in the world – he'd even been delighted to see Phil Bennett score a then Welsh record of 26 points. They wanted respect and that meant playing as hard and as well as we could. All but three of our 25-strong tour party were full Internationals.

The Japanese media was excited. Sumo wrestling was in decline, we learned, and rugby was on the up – although another of my favourites, baseball, introduced after the war by the Americans, was still the most popular sport with the public. The trip was to change our view of the country. I loved the place and the Japanese. I found the people very straightforward and honest. And who could fail to be impressed by the Bullet Train and the beauty of Mount Fuji?

The tour gave me my first chance to do a 'turn' in the bar, as was tradition then. Geoff 'The Ripper' Wheel and I always did 'There's a Hole in My Bucket'. We'd get a load of laughs – and get water all over the place. Everyone had something. Gareth, for instance, was a great singer and Bobby would rattle off endless jokes.

Some people say Geoff and I were in drag when we did our singing, but I don't remember that! I asked my wife if she thought that we did the song in drag and she said, "I've no idea. I've no idea what happened on tour!"

*

In Osaka we won by 56-12 and in Tokyo 82-6. Flattering scores against an inexperienced opposition? Maybe. The Japanese certainly had a disadvantage in height and weight at scrum and line-out, but they ran well and had some talent. However, we played absolutely lovely rugby, technically good and with flair. We never underestimated our opponent, never gave anything less than everything. Those training sessions in the heat in Bridgend paid off too – we were fit and committed to the 80 minutes. Spence and Dawes said afterwards that we were now the best side in the world, and who was to argue?

Osaka brought a special moment for me – a second try for Wales. Fenwick made a break and he passed it out to me, I ran about two yards and over the line. Sounds easy, but I'd say that's good support play! They'd said Fenwick wouldn't make it because he was on the small side, but he was skilful and committed; a good player and a good tackler.

Once again, it was a thrill for me to be picked out by JBG in an assessment of the tour:

> Modern rugby is based upon two vital factors: good possession and accurate and plentiful support.
>   One has only to note the manner in which prop Faulkner is seen at the side of the majority of scorers in the Japanese second Test to confirm the theory of support play.

That tour of Japan might seem like an aside, but it set us up for the season. As Carwyn James noted ahead of the 1976 Five Nations Championship, we could well be in for a Grand Slam with the seeds of victory "sown on Japanese soil".

Chapter Eight

"Up and under here we go"

BEING PART OF that Wales side made you a household name – although, strangely, I never thought of myself as famous. I just knuckled down and tried to keep my nose clean. Often our 'fame' went from the sublime to the slightly ridiculous. Around the same time as our dinner with the future King, we also got involved in a campaign for people to use their postcodes. 'The Dynamic Three train at NP4 8AX,' went one of the taglines. 'Please use your postcode.'

Most of my colleagues at the steelworks were fine with me being in the papers and on the television. You always had some jealous buggers, mind, but I used to ignore them. I didn't get into arguments. Wasn't worth it. I was the one in the Wales side, getting on the tours, working hard, so I ignored any of that jealousy. I'd walk past the people I knew who had snide words to say.

Before Wales games, we'd walk across to the stadium from the Angel Hotel and that was an amazing feeling. Clive Rowlands, then a selector, used to tell us not to stop for anybody on the way over or we'd never make it to the game in time. We signed autographs on the way back.

Mind you, we knew we weren't the *really* famous ones. It was the real stars who got the attention: Gareth Edwards, Phil Bennett, JPR – who were world-class players and true superstars. One time, Bobby came out of the Wales changing rooms and started to walk through the huge crowd. A man thrust out his autograph book. Bobby had only written B-O-B when the man said, "Oh, there's Gareth!" and grabbed the book back!

So we were always in the shadow of these superstars. We weren't in flashy roles, but we were happy to be a part of it. The big thing for us was the Pontypool Front Row thing: playing for Wales, playing for the Lions – that was the thing that made us special. Gave us a kind of aura. We were famous as a unit, a trio.

Max Boyce sang about us – 'Up and under here we go,' and the rest of it. I didn't take too much notice of it, but I met Max a few times. It was nice to be sung about, but it wasn't as big a part of my life as you might imagine. I didn't let that kind of attention affect me. It was the same with Bobby and Graham, to be honest. Pross told us not to let it go to our heads, and we listened to what Pross said. You might have arrived, he'd tell us, but it can all stop there. Keep thinking about your game.

With the fame came the demands of the game. They grew during the 1970s, especially in Wales. International rugby was now a TV spectacular. The Five Nations was live on the BBC on a Saturday afternoon. We had to keep fit through the season for our clubs in hard games, often out of the spotlight, but be ready for a series of hard, intense highs in the public eye.

Take the 1975/76 season: we'd had to go to Japan under pressure to win in the autumn, then take on Australia in the winter, and then do everything we could to win the Grand Slam in the spring. Everyone demanding success – not least ourselves. At Pontypool – and it would have been the same at Llanelli – there was pressure to maintain our grip on the domestic trophies too.

And while the Pontypool Front Row was dominating the International scene, the men we were coming up against week after week in Wales were no slouches. People like Colin Smart (later an England International and someone I'd coach at Newport), the Bridgend hooker Geoff Davies and his club skipper Meredydd James, Clive Williams at Aberavon, and Walter Williams and Glyn Shaw (who I'd replaced in the Wales team) at Neath. There were never easy games in the scrum. You had to give all you had, every time.

We'd struggled to have the same success in the Cup as we'd had in the League. In 1974 and 1975 we'd been knocked out in the semi-finals and quarter-finals by Llanelli, largely through the skill of their backs.

We got back from Japan to find that our clubmates had got off to a poor start, with a run of defeats – including a 34-4 hammering from Ebbw Vale – putting us at the bottom of the Merit Table, a table we'd topped the previous year. The Japanese tour coming at the start of the season had put us at a disadvantage, plus some of the boys had picked up early-season injuries. Anything that took the Pontypool Front Row out of the mix not only meant it was harder for our backs to get the ball, it made it harder for our boys to deny the opposition possession.

Just as we were trying to get back into club life, there was the further distraction of getting picked to play Australia in a match set to take place in Cardiff five days before Christmas. There was a sense of anticipation about the game against the Wallabies – and not all of it was good. So far on their tour, they had shown themselves fast with fists and boot studs. They were trying prove they were not the same side that had come over in 1966-67 and suffered a run of defeats.

Fifty thousand fans watched us dominate line-outs and rucks to record our biggest-ever win against the Aussies – 28-3. We won 80% of usable line-out ball and wheeled the scrum like demons to upset their possession. JJ scored three tries in the second half, and Gareth was immense. Again, I was pleased to hear that their tour manager, Ross Turnbull, had said the front row impressed him as a unit. However, they had their revenge on us in the new year when the Pontypool Front Row turned out for Gwent against the Aussies – and the men from Down Under won 15-26. But that was during the Five Nations – we had our minds on other things!

*

The thrills of 1975 and that success over Australia meant that expectations were high for the 1976 Five Nations Championship. We were on fire and the coming season would not disappoint.

But there was controversy ahead of the Championship when Phil Bennett was dropped and Aberavon's John Bevan brought in, with Swansea's David Richards as his reserve. By all accounts, Dawes hadn't told Phil in advance. It got messy when both Bevan and Richards got injured and Dawes and the selectors then had to go and ask Phil to play after all! It could have destroyed Benny, but I think it spurred him on.

The Press had the Cardiff matches against France and Scotland as 'home bankers', but felt the away matches against England and Ireland would be harder. We'd not won in Dublin since 1964 – although our captain, Merv, knew history was for being proved wrong. We approached every game with the same intent and respect for the opposition.

England were to be our first victims. For the match against the men in white we made our headquarters in the Kensington Palace Hotel. As usual with away games, we had to take a couple of days off work. The team and reserves met for training at Cardiff Arms Park after lunch on the Thursday, and then stayed at the Angel. The coach headed off after breakfast on Friday, crossing the border for the battle ahead. There was no training on a Friday, just an evening meal and the Prince of Wales Theatre. Saturday morning: team meeting at 11 a.m., lunch at 11.30 a.m., then leave the hotel before 1 p.m. Kick-off 2.30 p.m. After the game, we headed to the London Hilton for dinner and then the Grosvenor Hotel for the Anglo-Welsh Ball. The coach left for home at 11 a.m. on Sunday.

That's what our weekend looked like. No drinking before the match, of course, but a little after it.

On the field, we ran out 21-9 winners – our biggest winning margin at Twickenham up until then. JPR had a hell of game that day, bursting through with two tries from full back, despite having seven stitches in a gash in his cheek. But Merv was not impressed with the team display. Felt we were sluggish. It was the first game, Merv, give us a chance! Anyway, he told us to buck up.

And we did.

We beat Scotland in Cardiff 28-6 with the revived Benny kicking 13 points. Life in the ruck was vicious that day, but the Pontypool Front Row and Gareth Edwards – who scored a lovely late try – enjoyed hosting legends Ian McGeechan and Alastair McHarg on our table at the Angel Hotel afterwards.

And then it was off to Ireland with the Triple Crown within our grasp...

We stalled in the atmosphere whipped up by the Irish crowd and went behind 9-0. We came back to be a point ahead at the break, but we weren't convincing and Ireland were playing with real belief.

In the break, Merv gave us a tremendous earbashing and really ranted at us forwards to hold ourselves together. It worked, because in the space of a few minutes during the second half Phil, Gareth and Gerald all scored tries. We destroyed them, the papers said. They never put another point on the board. It was 34 to 9. Phil Bennett passed Barry John's scoring record.

And now the Grand Slam was on.

But first we had to beat an unbeaten French team. A massive game.

To be honest, I never really got nervous before a game, although there was always a sense of needing to be up to scratch: not only about playing well and winning this game, but about playing well enough that you would get picked for the next game too.

The man for nerves was Grav. He'd sit in the corner and literally start to shake. I remember before one game he was so nervous that we had to walk out of the changing room and leave him there. Physio Gerry Lewis always locked up, and he saw Grav behind the door. He had to go over and give him a shake and physically push him out of the room. Of course, Grav then came out onto the pitch at the tail end of the line of players and the crowd was roaring and he was alright after that: he had a brilliant game. He was a very emotional man, a lovely man, a man who was fanatical about Wales and playing for Wales.

But we all felt a touch of 'the Gravs' before that match against France. Only a touch, mind you. It was before a Cardiff crowd, after all. That said, we knew we were facing that incredibly strong French pack. We knew it was bound to be the hardest game of the season. And it was brutal too. Afterwards, French captain Jacques Fouroux had to deny they were a dirty team. Well, it was always dirty in the scrum.

The game was a whirl. I don't remember much about it. I know Benny picked up a knock early on but played on, with Steve Fenwick taking over for some of the place kicks. That's about it.

But I do remember that burst at the end. In the last seconds we were under pressure, France throwing everything at us, but we held them off. God, we fought. We weren't letting this get away. JPR saved a try with a bone-crushing shoulder charge, and we protected Gareth as he kicked to safety. We'd won, 19 points to 13.

A worldwide audience of sixty million watched the game on telly, seeing the Wales boys being jostled and patted on the back by jubilant supporters as they left the pitch. We hadn't always played our best rugby, but we'd shown character and that had seen us through. Clem Thomas and Geoffrey Nicholson's marvellous book *Welsh Rugby* says we won that grand slam "more grittily than prettily".

All the same, the sports pages loved us. The next day, the *Sunday Mirror* front page had us splashed all over it. *Glory Boys!* "It was breath-taking action from the moment the previously unbeaten French took an early lead to the final glory roars from the Welsh fans for Mervyn Davies and his magnificent men." I was really proud to read David Parry Jones quoting Mike Knill as saying I was the "best loosehead he'd seen".

Over the Championship we'd scored 102 points, a record for the Five Nations. We conceded only 37.

Well, what a high! Famous again!

But then back to work on Monday morning, with a tough club match midweek.

That year's dark moment came at our Cup semi-final against Swansea in Cardiff just three weeks later, when Mervyn Davies suffered a brain haemorrhage on the pitch. Merv recovered later but he didn't play again, and was a huge loss to rugby and to the Wales side especially. Merv was a great captain and a great man. He was intelligent, knew the right thing to say to motivate us, and was a great steadying influence in the pack when we started to get ragged.

We had to go on without him. To replace him as skipper, the WRU appointed Terry Cobner, who became the first Pontypool player to lead Wales since Clive Rowlands in 1963. The first fixture with Cob as captain was an autumn match against Argentina, an improving side, who were then just off the level played by International Rugby Board Tier 1 teams. We knew the Pumas were fit and up for a battle, but we probably underestimated them, or overestimated our own fitness and willingness to give 100% in the fixture. We certainly didn't fire on all cylinders as a side that day. Early season jitters, cobwebs left over after the summer, losing Merv – who knows.

In fact, we were trailing deep into injury time and the visitors were on the brink of making history for themselves, until JPR was hit by a short-arm tackle and Benny kicked the penalty. We scraped home to win by a point.

It was another one of those games where the WRU picked a full-strength squad but didn't consider it an International. The Argentinian players got a cap; we didn't.

But I had much bigger worries to come.

Chapter Nine

"You've got to bring Charlie out here!"

EVERY TIME YOU got picked for Wales you always had a letter, and you never knew whether you were in the squad until you had that letter. I didn't realise that until I got in the team, but from then on there was always that anxiety: have I been dropped or will I get to experience that feeling again? Everyone felt it.

I never took my Wales place for granted. And it's hard to realise now how much a cap meant. One cap back then was a massive honour. It was such a huge thing. It was like being picked to be the next James Bond. Everyone wanted to know you, everyone wanted to help you and be associated with you. Local garages would offer you cars at a discount. People wanted to be able to say I got a car for so-and-so, I got so-and-so a job.

But just when I was riding the crest of the wave with the lads, I came crashing down. There had been whispers about my age and pace and I'd heard them growing louder. To cut a long story short, I got dropped for the games against Ireland – the game in which Geoff Wheel and Willie Duggan became the first players sent off in Five Nations history – and France.

This was a blow, as no one worked harder than me to keep up their fitness. I trained every day of the week bar the day of a game. I mean, when they picked me in 1975, my age was irrelevant: I was capped because of my fitness. Because we were butties, I trained with Bobby and dragged him along every day. We'd take our kit to work and, in our break, we'd jump over the wall, run around Tredegar Park, up over the golf links, do a circuit and back – and we'd do it every day.

I trained like a dog. I even made things in work – weights which I hung on a leather belt over my neck to strengthen my neck muscles, because I knew that would be helpful in the front row. My contraptions made Bobby laugh!

"Charlie never stopped thinking about his fitness and strength," Bobby says. "He was always trying to improve himself, and that was good for me too."

At Pontypool we were the fittest club in Wales. And now the Welsh selectors were breaking up the Pontypool Front Row in red.

I watched as the Welsh scrum failed in Paris. The home team dominated. Merv wasn't there to steady the boys and I wasn't there to dig in my boots. Jean-Pierre Rives was on blistering form and a high tackle from Bastiat damaged Gerald Davies so badly he had to leave the field. We looked well out of it against a French team on the way to the title. The surprise defeat – our first in the Championship since Murrayfield in 1975 – meant the makers of *Grand Slam*, who were in Paris filming, had to rewrite the film's ending. If I'd been there, maybe they wouldn't have had to end the story with a defeat – who knows?

Graham was on the inside of events that day. He remembers:

Looking for a younger, more mobile model, the selectors dropped Charlie for the game against France in Paris. It was a mistake. Bobby was under so much pressure at the scrum – so low, because our loosehead was in trouble – that he couldn't strike with his foot and had no option but to hook the ball back with his head. That meant no 'channel one' quick ball for our brilliant backs, no 'channel two' ball either for our No. 8 and back row to work the very moves we'd planned in training during the week.

We lost 16-9. The Grand Slam had gone. They say you don't really appreciate someone until they're not there. In the changing rooms, our coach John Dawes approached Bobby and me to say, 'Don't worry, it won't happen again.'

After the game, I wondered if I'd get a phone call... And I did. They wanted me back for game three.

I wish I could tell you it was a happy ending, but 1977 was rough. I'd picked up a shoulder injury, wanted to work through it, but couldn't. My season was over.

It was devasting. The Five Nations Championship had become the highlight of the year. I was hungry for more caps. I was used to being part of the most exciting sports team on the planet. Only now I wasn't.

As Wales shuffled the pack in my absence – and still managed to win the Triple Crown again (which made me feel even worse) – there were now reports that my International career might be over completely. I wasn't having that. I ran up the hills of Gwent and around the track at Cwmbran Stadium, determined not just to get back to fitness but to get fitter than ever.

That summer I did a bit of coaching with the U19s, helping some future Internationals, but my sadness hung over me. And it was to deepen: that summer the Lions were due to tour New Zealand. My injury ruled me out of that too.

That hit me even harder. Bobby and Graham were going, and Terry Cobner too, and Gareth Evans, David Burcher and Jeff Squire from Newport.

I should be there too.

*

I followed some of the controversy about the Lions tour from home. They won their first game in the wind and cold but when the boys headed to the showers, their jubilation took a hit: there was no hot water in the visitors' dressing room!

Back on the pitch, the team struggled in some of the next few games, although by all accounts Graham was playing well. The first Test was lost; the second was won.

But there were problems for the squad. Bobby told me they were getting a lot of injuries because there was a lot of booting and stamping going on. He had to go propping for one game because there were no replacements. When Clive Williams of Aberavon suffered a knee injury, they called an emergency meeting.

The tour management called Bobby in and said, "Bob, we've got to bring a prop out. What do you think?"

Now, Bobby believed I'd have been there from the start if I'd been fully fit. He told them, "You've got to bring Charlie out here. Bring anyone else out and they'll know they're not going to get in the Test side, so it'll be a bit of a holiday. If Charlie comes, he will come out and *die* for you. He'll put everything into it."

Bobby waited outside the meeting. Phil Bennett came out and gave him the thumbs up. Bobby went straight to phone us in Newport. He told Jill, "Tell him to answer the phone as soon as it rings, because he's fucking coming out here."

I was over in Aberystwyth on a WRU coaching course when the call came. I was already thinking about a future in coaching. Injury had given me a taste of life without rugby and I didn't like it: whatever I did when I finally finished playing, I wanted to stay close to the game.

I'd worked my way back to fitness by training three or four times a week – on the weights, on the track at Cwmbran and running cross-country at Pontypool. I was desperate to get back to playing and knew that when the new season started at Pontypool, Terry, Bobby and Graham would be tired from the Lions tour and a lot of pressure would fall on my shoulders.

I'd also had it in the back of my mind that injuries on the tour might see me getting a call from John Dawes, who'd been appointed Lions coach.

And that's what happened.

It was the last day of the coaching course. I was just coming out of a maul on the training pitch when I saw Ray Williams waving at me.

"What is it?" I asked.

"You're going to New Zealand!" he shouted.

"What?!"

I'd come from being dropped by Wales a few months earlier to getting a call for what I felt was the greatest honour a British player could receive.

I was told to go home and pack. Back in Newport, the phone didn't stop ringing with messages of congratulations. *Thanks, boys, but I need to get out there.*

I felt the good wishes of Pontypool at my back and the fans' hopes that maybe the Pontypool Front Row would turn out for a Test for the Lions. It was the first time four Pontypool players would be on a Lions tour.

And then in that last week of July I was on a plane, spending long hours daring to dream of playing a Test. Deep down, I knew that was unlikely. I was just too late to the party.

There were only five matches left of the tour – and only two of them were Tests.

But I wasn't going there to make up the numbers. I was going to make myself seen and try to fight my way into the Test team. I'd had a bit of a rollercoaster ride: losing my place in the Wales team, fighting to get it back and then being struck down by injury and missing coveted caps. I didn't want to miss my one chance of playing for the Lions.

Before heading to London to catch my plane for New Zealand, I'd gone to Pontypool and run the grotto. There was no better preparation. I would have run all the way to New Zealand to have a chance of playing for the Lions.

*

I joined the boys in Dunedin – exhausted after travelling for about thirty hours to get there. Bobby was there to meet and look after me. He wrote that I said I'd arrived in "Dundee". He makes them all up, honestly! He likes to put a bit of colour into his stories. He was probably telling a few jokes at the time because Lions morale had slumped.

It was hard arriving in the middle of the tour, but I thoroughly enjoyed it. The boys were preparing for the third Test when I got there. It had pretty much rained the whole time they'd been out there, so it had become a test of endurance for them. I set about training to make a mark in the team, with the hope I'd win a place in the fourth and final Test. Cob was coaching the forwards, which was quite a coup for the Poolers.

The Viet Gwent appeared together for the first time on the tour at Pukekohe Stadium against Counties-Thames Valley. Against a team featuring five past, present and future All Blacks, we became the first club pack to represent the Lions. We were dominant and won easily. At some point, Bobby started a fucking big punch-up. It was hilarious, actually. He walloped somebody and suddenly everybody was fighting... except their bloke running with the ball and poor old Mike Gibson chasing him!

The Pontypool Front Row missed the next game and were back in for the final provincial match – another victory, this time against the Bay of Plenty at Rotorua. I was very pleased that we'd won both games where I'd been in the team with Graham and Bobby. Success in the two games where the PFR became the Lions front row.

But a spot in the final Test just eluded me. Despite coming out late and playing catch-up, though, it was a close-run thing. I was playing well, training hard and, afterwards, I got

77

called aside by George Burrell, the Scottish manager of the tour, who said if I'd been out there a bit longer, they would have picked me for the Test side.

There was some small consolation. We flew up to Fiji for the final game and the Pontypool Front Row played in that one. Although sadly we lost in the blazing heat of Suva.

I made the long flight home filled with some regret. To go all that way and not play in one of the big games. Shame, that. Big disappointment. It would have been a dream to play New Zealand in a Test match for the Lions.

Chapter Ten

"You carry water for other people to drink"

1978. ELATION. TRIPLE Crown. Grand Slam...

...but also the bitterest defeat of my whole life. A disappointment – an anger – that's never gone away.

Anyway, first things first.

I remember one hell of a battle with Cardiff early in the 1977/78 season. They were unbeaten when they came to Pontypool, and we threw everything at them in the second half after going into the break 9-0 down. I was in the pack with Brian Gregory and Eddie Butler and we fought like rabid tigers, but we missed two penalties and they scored one late on. We couldn't get back and lost 12-6.

But the spirit we showed that night kept going. I think I was acting skipper some of the time, and I enjoyed that. In November we played Neath at home. Our mauls were like steamrollers. We bent their scrum like folding paper. Bobby, Graham and I were relentless: even as the points stacked up against the visitors, we kept at them. Demoralised them. Shattered them. The final score? 51-0. One of the finest performances of a team I played in.

Funnily enough, here's a true story: during the game I found a pound note blowing across the pitch. Normally, that would have been worth keeping in those days. But, no, I handed it to the ref. I didn't need it. That performance was reward enough!

In *The Good, The Bad and The Ugly* by Nick Bishop and Alun Carter, Mike Ruddock recalled playing as a teenager for Tredegar against us that season, when they tried out a front three in the scrum. He said he came out of the scrum as if he'd "been through a threshing machine".

Yes, relentless – that was definitely the word for the Pontypool Front Row.

That said, the issue for Pontypool was that when the Five Nations came around, it tended to rip the guts out of the team, with both the PFR and Cob on national duty.

Come the 1978 Championship, Bobby was like a wild dog on the leash. He was determined to get the better of England's Peter Wheeler, who had replaced him in the Lions Test team.

We got the better of them, but it wasn't pretty. The rain ruined that game. But even in the wind, Gareth kicked downfield beautifully, again and again, to ease pressure and put them on the defence. We won 9-6, with all our points coming from Benny's boot. It was the first time we hadn't scored a try at Twickenham since the early 1960s. But it was points in the bag.

Come 18 February, snow and icy conditions put paid to most of Britain's sporting calendar. But our game against Scotland in Cardiff went ahead – in a blizzard. We won the toss but gave the visitors the wind advantage in the first half and hoped to hold our own. We did more than that and went in at half-time just ahead. We let them off the hook towards the end of the second half but still ran out winners, 22-14, with Grav and Derek Quinell scoring their first Wales tries.

The blizzard continued after the final whistle, trapping players and spectators from Scotland and down west in the pubs and hotels of Cardiff for several days.

Ireland at Lansdowne Road was a tougher prospect, and it turned out to be a bitter and brutal physical battle. Gareth Edwards called it the toughest game he ever played in. For

Tony Faulkner, better known to the rugby world as Charlie.

Young Charlie in the arms of his mother, Ivy.

Class photo at Father Hills school in Newport. Charlie is to the right of the headteacher.

Charlie enjoying judo with his brothers Clive (left) and Roger (centre).

Charlie loved his days in the Territorial Army.

The Whitehead's squad. Charlie is front right, with a Teddy Boy haircut, and Bobby Windsor is behind him.

Bobby and Charlie claiming a try, in a game for Whitehead's against Bassaleg in 1968.

Charlie in his mid twenties.

Charlie and Jill on their wedding day, 1968.

At Newport Saracens. Charlie is second from the right at the back.

The Gwent team which played New Zealand in 1972.

harlie with his first child, Jayne,
orn in 1972.

Charlie with his guiding light, Pontypool
coach Ray Prosser.

ontypool Rugby Club, Merit Table winners 1972/73. Charlie is fourth from the right
t the back.

Squad photo for the 1974 Crawshay's tour to Cornwall. Charlie is fourth from the right, third row.

The Pontypool Front Row at Pontypool Park.

In the line-out for Pontypool. Charlie is third from the left.

The Pontypool Front Row after a game, victory smiles on their faces.

The Pontypool Front Row celebrating afterwards. Long before Ant and Dec, they always got into the right position to be photographed.

Fe welwch y tri yn sgarmesu yn NP4 8AX

Defnyddiwch eich Cod Post

Campaigners: the Pontypool Front Row encouraging people to use their postcodes.

Cartoonists loved the Pontypool Front Row, and this cracker has Terry Cobner too.

Debut day: the Wales team to play France in 1975. A proud Charlie is fourth from the right at the back.

Picked for the Barbarians' Easter tour, 1975.

WELSH RUGBY UNION

Royal London House,
28/31, St. Mary Street, 28th April 1975.
Cardiff,
CF1 2PP.

Dear Tony,

Congratulations on your selection as a member of the touring team to visit Japan in September next. We are looking forward to a very happy and successful tour and hope that during the coming summer you will keep reasonably fit.

Our first get-together will be on Sunday 18th May at the National Sports Centre, Sophia Gardens, where we will have our first briefing.

Kind regards.

Yours sincerely,

L.M. Spence
Hon. Manager

S.J. Dawes,
Hon. Assistant Manager

Letter congratulating Charlie on being picked for the tour of Japan.

WELSH RUGBY UNION TOUR OF JAPAN
SEPTEMBER 1975

A・G・フォークナー

プロップ
製鋼所勤務

Charlie's business card for the Japan tour – the first line in Japanese is his surname, the second 'prop' and the third 'works in a steel mill'.

The squad to tour Hong Kong and Japan, 1975. Charlie is on the left at the back.

Playing in Japan.

Keeping up with JPR in Japan.

The Gwent squad to face Australia, January 1976. Charlie is third from the left.

The Committee of the Welsh Rugby Union has pleasure in informing

A. G. Faulkner

that he has been selected to play for Wales against England at Cardiff on Saturday, 5ᵗʰ March 1977

Yours faithfully,

W. H. Clement

SECRETARY

PONTYPOOL prop Tony Faulkner is in no doubt where he is going. Next stop New Zealand says the card he is holding up—and this means a 12,000-mile trip to join the British Lions on Monday as a replacement for Clive Williams.

I'll be fighting for Test place says Faulkner

Dropped from the Wales team at the start of the 1977 Five Nations, Charlie gets a recall for the England match in March.
Sadly, injury keeps him out of the game.

The *South Wales Argus* reports Charlie's Lions call-up.

A cartoon celebrates Charlie's return to the Wales squad.

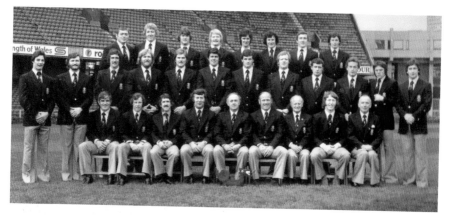

The Wales team to tour Australia in 1978. Charlie is on the left at the back.

Charlie's programme for that controversial game against New Zealand, 1978, and the official programme for Wales v France, 1979 – Charlie's last match for Wales.

Coaching the Sarries. Charlie's success there leads to the job at Newport RFC.

TONY FAULKNER GETS NEWPORT COACHING JOB

by Stephen Bale

TONY FAULKNER, hero of many a successful campaign with Wales and Pontypool, has accepted the daunting challenge of restoring Newport to the pinnacle on which they once familiarly stood year after year.

The appointment of British Lion Faulkner as Newport coach with special responsibility for the forwards, brings a happy return to Rodney Parade for a man who as a player twice unsuccessfully had trials with Newport in the sixties.

He gets the job after less than a season coaching

reputation second to none in Gwent, and their success was vividly demonstrated when Newport struggled so badly against a combined Newport High School Old Boys-Newport Saracens side in a centenary game in March.

After being turned down as a player by Newport, loose head prop Faulkner went on to Cross Keys and thence to Pontypool, where he formed part of the fabled front row with Bobby Windsor and Graham Price.

Injury

He won 19 caps for Wales between 1975-79 and was

Geoff Evans and Roy Cadland are two recently retired players who have indicated that they are after a committee place and Faulkner will automatically get a committee seat as coach?

The new rugby committee are expected to meet for the first time in early June. Their first decision will be on a new captain, a job for which Colin Smart and Kerry Williams are the clear front runners.

Squad

Newport have picked a powerful squad including two Welsh internationals, Gareth Evans and Robert Ackerman, for tomorrow's Caldicot seven-a-side tournament

Taking the coaching job at Newport.

Publicity photo from Charlie's brewery days.

RUGBY HERO GETS BABY TO SAFETY

Christian crusade at 'Satanic' threat

GWENT rugby legend Charlie Faulkner has told how he carried a baby 100 yards to safety through a stampeding crowd after a suspected terrorist attack at Jerusalem's Wailing Wall.

Thousands of people panicked when a tear gas canister exploded at the closing ceremony of Israel's Maccabiah Games — the Jewish Olympics.

As people rushed to escape, the former Pontypool and Wales prop forward spotted that a small pushchair had been tipped over.

Despite suffering the effects of the tear gas, Mr

"I took it to the police who reunited the baby with its mother. I was impressed because the baby did not cry once," said Mr Faulkner, aged 58, of Craig Park Hill, Maybee, Newport.

The 58-time prop forward, who won 19 caps for Wales in the fifties and now works as a representative of Welsh Brewers, described the events at Jerusalem as a "frightening riot."

He said: "It was a terrible thing. Women were being sick and a lot of people could have been killed in the stampede."

Mr Faulkner, who described the Great British rugby side to a silver medal at the games, was at the Wailing Wall with about 4,000 athletes and spectators enjoying the closing ceremony of the games when the tear gas canister exploded.

Events at the closing ceremony of the Maccabiah Games make the news.

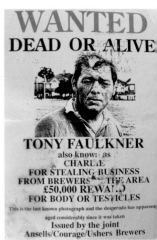

WANTED
DEAD OR ALIVE

TONY FAULKNER
also known as
CHARLIE
FOR STEALING BUSINESS
FROM BREWERS IN THE AREA
£50,000 REWARD
FOR BODY OR TESTICLES

This is the last known photograph and the desperado has apparently
aged considerably since it was taken
**Issued by the joint
Ansells/Courage/Ushers Brewers**

Charlie was doing so well at Whitbread that his colleagues had this poster drawn up.

Two Charlies!

Charlie and Jill during a holiday in Bermuda.

Charlie with good friends Paddy Burke (left) and John Blackborow.

Charlie and Jill's children: Jayne, Jason and Laura.

Charlie and Jill's grandchildren: Mali, Libby, Leo, Lois, Logan and Nia.

Sharing a laugh with Bobby Windsor as he entertains with one of his stories.

Charlie and Jill walking back to their holiday home in Spain during one of their last visits there.

us, in the rucks and mauls, it was the kind of match you know you've been in for a week or so afterwards.

I think one of the reasons we stayed in the game was the pressure of the Pontypool Front Row and the controlled feeding of the ball at the back of the scrum. Fenwick scored four penalties and a try – fed by Pricey from the ruck.

All the same, we were pretty dead on our feet with a few minutes to go and the scores level at 16-16.

As we prepared for a scrum, Gareth looked us in the eye. We could tell he was feeling it. But there was something in his eyes. "Come on!" he said. "One last effort, boys!"

We went down, put everything into it and felt the Irish moving backwards. The ball came out to Gareth and eventually to JJ, who flew over for the try.

20-16.

As Graham says:

Charlie, Bobby and myself had successful individual careers, but together we became a unit that was greater than the sum of the parts, and that showed that day. We shunted the Irish eight backwards. In that one moment they seemed to deflate, fall apart, while our players grew in stature and we went on to win a triple Triple Crown.

Back in the changing room, we all slumped on the benches for some time, too exhausted even to pull our jerseys over our heads. But the prime ribs and potatoes at the after-match dinner at the Shelbourne Hotel went down well – even though our own ribs were pretty bruised and battered!

A third Triple Crown in a row for Wales – the first country to do that – and my second. We flew back into Cardiff and for me our arrival was one of the greatest moments of my career. There were thousands of people at the airport. It was sheer adulation. You expect it in the ground but to see people on the streets was amazing. They were standing twenty deep. I felt like a film star – we all did.

France came to Cardiff for the Grand Slam decider. Old foes, big names, one of the best back rows in the business: Jean-Claude Skrela, Jean-Pierre Bastiat and Jean-Pierre Rives. And their front row was formidable too: the bruiser Gérard Cholley, Alain Paco, Robert Paparemborde. Skrela and Bastiat were bowing out of International rugby and they'd won the previous three matches of the Championship: they wanted this Grand Slam.

But the fans in Westgate Street wearing the red jerseys and waving the Welsh flags wanted it too.

Both Gerald Davies and I struggled to recover from injury for the game. Gerald had injured a hamstring and wasn't fit in time, while I'd jarred my neck against Ebbw Vale. But our scrummaging had kept us in that game against Ireland and there was *no way* I was going to miss playing France.

I worked every day to get fit, and was ready.

On the day, Phil Bennett had his greatest game for Wales, scoring two tries. One came when we pushed the French pack off the ball.

Pricey has said that I was the only loosehead prop to get the better of Paparemborde, perhaps the best and strongest tighthead the sport has ever seen:

> Charlie was able to force his head under the Frenchman and then bore into the most vulnerable area in the upper body, the side of the ribcage near the floating ribs. At his peak, Charlie was the most ruthless loosehead scrummager I have ever played with or against.

I remember Gareth Edwards landed a perfect drop goal. We won 16-7 and had the Grand Slam that the French had denied us the season before.

Dawes said afterwards that we had to be one of the greatest rugby sides of all time.

That's when we got our invitation to 10 Downing Street to meet Prime Minister James Callaghan (who was MP for

Cardiff South-East) and former PMs Harold Wilson and Ted Heath. Sir Geraint Evans was there too, so we soon burst into *'Hen Wlad Fy Nhadau'*.

The WRU President, T Rowley Jones, said of us, "Not only are they a great team but they are great men and great Welshmen. They are a credit to Wales in every sense."

High praise.

But this is sport. You win one thing, but the game goes on.

We were to realise we weren't as invincible as we thought we were when we headed Down Under later that year.

The day after the France game, Gareth announced that he was retiring from International rugby. What a player and what a man. A genuine sporting legend. He played for Wales over 11 seasons and went on three Lions tours. Benny stepped down too – marking, I suppose, the first signs that a special era was nearing its end.

*

Over the years I've always felt the Welsh pack as a whole didn't get the credit it deserved. There was a moment in the 1978 Grand Slam win against France which summed that up.

It was a French put-in at a scrum in their 22, and we pushed them back off the ball and took it against the head. Quinnell fed Gareth and he whipped it out to Benny, who went over.

Everyone talked about Benny jinking through for the try – and they did for years afterwards – but they never mention the pack pushing France off the ball. Now, France didn't like being pushed back, so for them to lose one against the head and concede a try was a big thing. It was a try that put us back in the game.

I look back and think we made a vast contribution there. I remember saying to Pross at the time it was a bit upsetting that they didn't even mention us.

He said, "Charlie, you are in a position where you carry water for other people to drink."

I thought that was a bloody good way of putting it.

*

Wales toured Australia in 1978 with myself, Bobby and Graham in the squad and Terry Cobner as captain. As Graham has said, we had our eye on bringing Jeff Squire over from Newport to Pontypool and, as Bobby was in charge of allocating rooms to players, he made sure Jeff was rooming with him. Bobby spent every spare moment telling Jeff how brilliant Pross and Pontypool were and what a grand life it was, or something like that. Bobby can talk. And when Jeff escaped Bobby, he was faced with Cob, Graham or me having a word, giving it the big sell. It's surprising we didn't frighten him off, but our enthusiasm for Pross and the club must have impressed him and he joined us soon after.

We flew to Australia in May. That Aussie tour brought us back to earth with a jolt after the Grand Slam. We racked up injuries (including Cob), still felt exhausted after a punishing Five Nations, and the players who'd been on the Lions tour had by this point been playing pretty much relentlessly for about eighteen months. The refs were also, well, very Australian. Not too neutral, I'd say.

We lost both Tests, in Brisbane (18-8) and Sydney (19-17), although we won the majority of the other games. Pricey got knocked out in Sydney after getting clouted from behind. No one got punished. I'd also swear that one of their kicks missed the post, but the ref gave it.

The Wallabies taught us a valuable lesson: we were beatable. We were outplayed for pace and, frustratingly, determination. Had we won too much back home? Were we jaded? I don't know. Our young players took the greatest hammerings, I think. Cob captained well, Graham, Bobby and I scrummaged fiercely, and Gerald and JPR showed flashes of their usual brilliance. Perhaps most importantly, we discovered a new half-back partnership: Terry Holmes and Gareth Davies.

But whatever the individual performances, we were a team that lost. We were losers. A hard bump back to earth.

Off the pitch, I got to hook up with an old friend, John Blackborow, from Newport. John had been playing for Newbridge when I was playing for Cross Keys and he'd been to school with Bobby. In fact, when Bobby and I had been playing for Whitehead's, John had been one of the first to encourage us to move to the Sarries. Anyway, John was then playing for a club out in Oz, and he took us out for a marvellous day on his boat.

We went off around Sydney Harbour, past the Opera House and the Australian Navy base. It was quite a group: Clive Davis, who'd played alongside John at Newbridge, JPR, Terry Holmes, Stuart Lane, Gerald Davies and Steve Fenwick. And Mike 'Spike' Watkins was there too. And when we anchored off one of the well-known nudist beaches, he was the only one brave enough to swim ashore!

We left Spike there and sailed around. When we returned an hour or so later to pick him up, we could see him signing autographs. His Welsh-white skin stood out among the Aussie suntans!

*

There was no sunshine at the Arms Park on 11 November of that year, though. A day to forget. A day you *can't* forget.

It was the day New Zealand came to Cardiff. Wales had played the All Blacks ten times by then, including that no-cap game in 1974. The Kiwis had won seven of the games and we hadn't beaten them since 1953. We needed the rub of the green. We weren't to get it.

We had a few changes. Gerald had retired after Australia, so JJ Williams switched to the right wing. Terry Holmes came in for Gareth Edwards, and Gareth Davies was also in.

We knew that playing against the All Blacks was always hell. They would run over you like a steam train. They'd trample you into the dirt. If you were on the floor, you were dead meat. I'll tell you what, back in our day, you *never* went to the ground on purpose.

That day, though, our forward play had helped us get the better of them, earning us penalties by Davies and Fenwick. It was 25 years since we'd beaten the All Blacks and we were just about to do it.

With minutes to go we were up 12-10...

...and then the ball went into touch on our 25.

It was our throw. It was taken, but was called again. As we prepared for it, I saw their second rows Andy Haden and Frank Oliver chatting together.

Scheming, I should say.

Anyway, when the throw came in, they both dived out of the line-out and to the floor as if they'd been barged. I even heard them scream. The crowd couldn't hear it because of their own noise, but we heard it.

English referee Roger Quittenton awarded a penalty against us and – as the home crowd nearest the action, who'd seen what had happened, booed – Brian McKechnie slotted the penalty between the posts. That scheming and Quittenton's judgement cost us the game.

We'd won all the rucks, all the line-outs. It had been a comparatively easy game, considering it was the All Blacks. We had a good side, a good pack. I don't know if they were below par, but we certainly played our hearts out and were on top.

It was the hardest defeat to deal with in my career. Not a day goes by where I don't think of it. My worst moment for Wales. It was terrible.

But, for me, the All Blacks didn't get satisfaction out of that game. They had more points than us, but that was it. We were the better team. We out-rucked them, out-scrummed them, we beat them in the line-outs. We deserved to win.

Afterwards, we sat there not talking. Jill came down to the Angel and said she wished she hadn't bothered. Nobody could look anyone in the eye. We looked at the floor. I felt sick, to be honest. Sometimes you lose and you know they were better. But we felt cheated.

There was a dinner, of course. Everyone was quiet – there was none of the normal chat between opponents. When you lose fair and square, in the evening you shake their hands, have a few beers and know they played well. That's the name of the game.

The Welsh selectors went round us saying they didn't want any confrontation.

Quittenton was there and he was given a bit of stick by some of our boys. I couldn't look him in the eye. It was a blatant scheme and he'd fallen for it.

I spoke to him later when he was refereeing at London Welsh and I was coaching Newport. He never accepted it as a mistake to me. I think he felt the Welsh needed taking down a peg. That's what I think. I've seen it written that Quittenton saw Geoff Wheel's hand on Oliver's shoulder as they jumped at the front of the line-out, but it was never enough for what happened.

Later on, I had a few drinks with McKechnie, who'd kicked the winning penalty. It was a couple of seasons later and I bumped into him in Cardiff. We went into a pub and had quite a few beers. Over the four hours, I couldn't help coming back to that moment in the game, but he shrugged it off. I mean, he understood what had happened but he said you have to take your opportunities, and that was it. All's fair in love and war, sort of thing. But I know some of those New Zealand boys regretted what happened that day.

And Andy Haden's autobiography confirmed the scheming I knew I'd witnessed before the line-out. In *Boots 'n' All* he said the action was "premeditated" and "born of desperation on the spur of the moment".

Hmmm, yes. They'd been outjumped throughout the game and they spotted a way to change that.

Not on.

Chapter Eleven

Exit the Dragon

EVERYTHING WAS CHANGING.

Gareth Edwards was gone, Phil Bennett too. JPR replaced Gareth as captain but he was to be much harder to replace as a player. After all, Gareth had made more than fifty consecutive appearances at scrum half for us. Incredible dominance of a role. Gareth Davies and Terry Holmes had been blooded as replacements on the tour of Australia, but the Five Nations would be a different kind of pressure. Fans were already thinking the golden era was over. We'd spent the winter watching slow-motion replays of Haden's Oscar-worthy dive. Predictions of rugby disaster – a national pastime – were everywhere.

The gloom-mongers nodded along to themselves at half-time in our first game, when we went in 13-6 at Murrayfield.

But an Elgan Rees try settled us and set us on the road to a 19-13 victory, with Terry scoring at the end. It was a tough match, played in a great spirit. Our pack performed well. J B G Thomas said it was the pack's victory, and we were praised by the opposition. It was the forwards who pushed Scotland off the ball and drove over the line for the winning try.

After those matches against Australia and the All Blacks, it was a relief to get things going again for the fans.

Back in Cardiff, Ireland again pushed us hard, tackling like demons. I had great respect for their forwards, players like Phil Orr, Pa Whelan and Ginger McLoughlin. But

Fenwick wore his golden boot, kicking four penalties and two conversions, and we got the better of them – just: 24-21. Ireland had never scored that many points in a match and still lost.

And so to Paris, the scene of my debut in 1975. We'd won then, but things looked different now.

Whereas in 1975 all the changes had been made before the tournament, we now felt like a squad in transition during the Championship. Or that's what it felt like to me. Nobody's fault. That uneasiness and an injury to Geoff Wheel meant we were underdogs for the press. Facing us down: Paparemborde, Paco and Vaquerin, three units of 16 stone of meanness. All heavier than any of us three in the Pontypool Front Row. We lost by a point – 14-13 – but in truth we were well beaten.

It's so painful to say that. Not because it's not true or because I don't like to admit we were second best, but because it was to be my last game for Wales.

I had a troublesome knee injury that I'd picked up at a Welsh Cup game against Cardiff and couldn't shake. It started to really affect my training and all the extra things I liked to do to maintain higher fitness.

The selectors decided not to risk me for the England game and brought in John Richardson of Aberavon for his first full cap. Physio Gerry Lewis told me if they hadn't made the decision to replace me, it would have been touch and go right up to the whistle as to whether I'd have been fit.

The headlines were hard to read. *Injured Faulkner out of Welsh side. Famous Pontypool Front Row to be parted.*

It was devastating. I was looking at the end: I was 38 – although still 36 officially. Right up to the end, the match-day programmes listed my birth year as two years after it really was!

In the end, Bobby missed the England game too. We had to watch our boys recover in the final quarter and score five tries to win 27-3 – our fourth Triple Crown in a row.

But the curtain was down on the Super Seventies. J J Williams wrote in his memoir that when he looked around the dressing room that day, he realised how much had changed. Only JPR remained from JJ's debut in 1973.

The 1970s were a golden age for Wales. I was fortunate to be at the heart of the second half of that. To witness, first-hand, the jinking genius of Gerald Davies, Gareth Edwards and Phil Bennett, JJ's grace, the runs of JPR...

And then there was us in the pack.

The Viet Gwent had played 19 Internationals together. But only Graham – ten years younger than me – would continue in a Wales shirt. JPR was thinking of hanging up his boots. Gareth Edwards, Phil Bennett and Gerald Davies were already gone. JJ retired after the England match.

For me, it had all been very special. I'd worked so hard for my caps and waited so long, struggling in the mud and rain and blood for my chance.

All my caps had come in my mid and late thirties. That made it sweet. I was proud of that. Proud that my fitness had always got me through. I was happy with the contribution I'd made.

But, let me tell you, it's pretty tough to realise you aren't going to hear that roar of the crowd any more. Those 50,000 voices raised in song, or to urge the pack forward. The waves of sound and emotion which would pass over you from the supporters. No, not pass over you: run right through you, gather in your veins, pump your heart and urge you on.

Yes, it's pretty hard to lose that, and to know it won't come again.

The Pontypool Front Row had been lauded as the best front row ever. Maybe we were – it's not for us to say. Most of the time we felt we got on top of the opposition, but no-one wins every time. Bobby talks about a game we played for East Wales against Argentina, and that was a day we were outplayed for sure. Not one I like to be reminded of.

When my International career came to an end, Newport MP Roy Hughes sent me a letter. "You have achieved great distinction and all supporters of Welsh rugby are proud of you. Certainly, the Pontypool Front Row will be talked about for many years hence."

He wasn't wrong.

As the 1980s started, I turned 39. My days in the sunshine were gone – if that was the way I chose to look at it.

I didn't.

I played the last of my 210 games for Pontypool against Abertillery in November 1980 (although I was to join up with Graham and Bobby again three years later for a charity match) and turned my mind to the future.

There'd been plenty of great days. Amazing matches. But it was time for something new.

*

All this time, I'd still been working for Whitehead's. I decided to make a change and when I saw a sales rep job advertised for the brewery, Whitbread, I thought I'd try for that. The boss was Vernon Spragg, a very down-to-earth fellow. He said, "There's something about you I like. I'll give you a three-month trial, and see what you're made of."

He told me I'd have my own patch, where there'd be so many pumps in so many pubs and I'd have to meet targets. Make sure beer was drunk, more pumps were put on. They even put targets on us for getting our payments in. Anyway, I went at it.

My old Wales butties helped me a bit, actually. We'd been asked to record some songs – favourites like 'Sloop John B' and 'Green Green Grass of Home' for an album called *The Other Side of the Dragon*. Everyone was going to be heading to the Rockfield Studios in Monmouth for a couple of days' singing. The producers were uniting us all – JPR, Gerald,

Benny, JJ, Gareth, the Pontypool Front Row, Merv, Derek Quinnell... plus Delme Thomas, John Taylor, Paul Ringer, Barry John and John Dawes.

Now, I was hoping to get the British Legion Club in Monmouth to stock my beer, so I figured a visit from this star-studded line-up of Welsh legends could help. The first day was rehearsals, so afterwards I invited all the boys to the club, where I'd ordered a buffet be laid on. The night turned into cabaret with everyone singing, and a full barrel of beer disappeared down our throats.

The following day we returned to the studio for the actual recording. We were all rough as can be. We started on the second barrel and worked through that as we recorded the album. And the legion? Well, yes, they loved their night with the stars and started to stock my beer.

Mr Spragg loved how I worked. After three months he told me, "You've got the job – we're very pleased with you."

When I went and sat down for my first sales meeting, I was the only one out of the ten there who was non-academic. All the rest were out of university or college. But I put them all to shame: I opened up so many new accounts that I used to keep the team going! It wasn't because of charm or intelligence, it was because – just like in my rugby days – I used to put the effort in. I went at it every night of the week. I made a point of being successful at it.

But I wasn't one of those reps who gave it all the patter, because the publicans used to be fed up with them. They used to see those smart-talkers all the time. I took a different approach, not going for the hard sell. "How are you doing? Is everything selling okay? What about the lager compared with the beer?"

It got so that I would be sent to different areas where sales were low. I'd move around Gloucester, Cardiff, Newport. I was like a fireman, if you know what I mean. I did 23 years for Whitbread and was always happy there.

Now, I know the fact that I was a Wales rugby player contributed to the impact on people when they met me, but I never promoted it. I never said, "I'm Charlie Faulkner and I played for Wales." No, I never went down that line. They probably knew who I was, but I never, ever promoted it. They weren't going to take a bad deal just because I was a Wales rugby player, anyway. I still had to do the business.

What being 'Charlie Faulkner' did for me was open doors, I suppose. They wanted to meet you. But once they'd shaken your hand, what they wanted was a good deal on the beer!

*

Despite the new career, being without rugby just wasn't going to happen. I'd loved doing my training courses, loved learning everything there was about propping, and I knew coaching was the way forward for me.

Nothing was going to replace playing but I relished the chance to coach. To discipline and mould a squad of players, to inspire them with my own dedication to fitness and training. And most importantly to continue to spread the secrets to the art of the scrum.

I dipped my toe into coaching with the Special Air Service regiment rugby team who I knew through the TA, and I'd keep that going. But the first proper coaching job I went to was at my old club, Newport Saracens. It was good to be back with them. My old friend John Blackborow was playing there. He'd actually been looking to leave, but stayed when he realised I was coming. Blackie has boxed and all sorts, so he knows a bit about fitness.

"Charlie got us extremely fit and set us up as a well-organised team," John says. "Anybody late for training had a few words in both ears."

John's as tough as can be and he loved my methods of training. But not everyone did. They thought it was too hard.

And one night I watched one boy walking off... and I couldn't help myself. I strode across the grass, my breath in the air, lit by the floodlights. I was angry.

I found the lad in the dressing room and I told him in no uncertain terms that no-one walks off the pitch when I'm running a training session. By the time the rest of the boys came in behind us, I'd lifted the fella up and placed him on one of the coat hooks.

The lad took it well, to be fair. We had a chuckle about it later... And he didn't walk off again, either.

I managed to get the Sarries from a team that couldn't win a game to a respected outfit in six months. We actually went three months without a defeat. When we had a short tour to Bordeaux, the French put out a strong side for us. I think they thought I was bringing half the Wales team over.

Our success got noticed – especially when our forwards put on one hell of a performance in a friendly against Newport. After just a season, the Newport RFC committee came calling for me with an offer I couldn't refuse: to coach at a higher level with my hometown team, and take special responsibility for the forwards.

Except I knew it was going to be a challenge. The Black and Ambers were well in the doldrums.

Chapter Twelve

"I'll only play for Charlie Faulkner RFC"

A "DAUNTING CHALLENGE" – that's what the *South Wales Argus* called what lay ahead of me at Newport. It would need a lot of work to restore the club to its former glory.

For the 1981/82 season the Black and Ambers had brought in a slew of new players – and me. Our new line-up included Wales 'B' scrum half Leighton O'Connor, who never really worked out and didn't last half the season with us; David Fryer; centre Mark Fenwick, brother of Steve; outside half Mike Goldsworthy; full back Mike Morgan; and Wales International back row Stuart Lane. I tried to coax David Bishop to join us, but Pross took him from under my nose.

The big one for me personally, though, was Wales 'B' hooker Mike 'Spike' Watkins. I really wanted to get him to Rodney Parade.

I called Spikey the "rubber ball" because he always bounced back. In 1979 he'd been on the verge of his debut for Wales when he'd gone out on a session with Jeff Davies. The 'Hookers Night Out', the Press later called it. It ended in a scuffle with Cardiff police and Spike got dropped by Wales and suspended by Cardiff. It was a scandal.

In 1981 he was still at Cardiff, but I didn't think he was happy. As he said himself later in his book, *Spikey*, he felt he was getting picked for all the hard games but being sidelined for the easier fixtures and so he wasn't getting a chance to be seen at his best and most dominant. Llanelli had approached Spike and offered him the vice-captaincy – a pretty decent offer – but as Spike worked as a lorry driver, travelling all over, being based at a club down west didn't really suit him.

I wanted him at Newport but there was a big problem: while Spike loved the supporters, he couldn't take to the committee. That was Spikey summed up!

Spike had been Bobby's understudy at hooker for Wales and I always thought he was a good player. I reckoned I could make him a great player at Newport. To lure him, I bought some nice biscuits and invited him up to the house for a chat. He knew what it was about, so I didn't beat about the bush.

"Join me at Newport RFC, Spike."

He turned me down flat. "I can't stand the place," he said. I suppose we were a big come-down from the glamour of Llanelli. We didn't have a lot going for us. Spike didn't even like our jerseys! I kept him talking, appealing, but it was no good. He'd made up his mind before he'd come. He just wanted a chat and a biscuit.

I saw him to the door but, as he was leaving, I had a thought. I knew Spike didn't like the Newport committee, but he wasn't the kind of guy to like committee suits anywhere. And, anyway, all players disagreed with committee decisions from time to time – sometimes a bit more often than that!

I also knew, though, that Spike *did like me*.

"Spike, what if you don't play for Newport?" I called after him. "What if you come and play for *me*?"

Spike hesitated, then nodded and held out his hand. As he wrote later, "And that's how I came to play for Charlie Faulkner RFC, and not Newport."

Spike and I are great friends, and I knew he was there for me, but when I saw that line in his book, I was moved – really touched. Over those early seasons at Newport, I made it one of my key aims to keep improving Spike's play in the pack and make sure he caught the eye of the Wales selectors.

The Newport team was a young squad with plenty of potential. They'd lost a lot of games in the previous season by narrow margins and, for me, the main problem I'd seen was a lack of fitness. Therefore, I had them up at the pitch at St Julian's school, running up and down these steep banks. Alun Williams, who joined us later, says these banks were my Newport version of the Pontypool grotto run!

I felt a bit like Pross, starting everything from the pack, putting the rugby roles I knew best right at the centre of my planning. I wanted a front five which was not only an effective ball-winning unit, but also a hardened group that wouldn't be intimidated by the reputations of Pontypool and Swansea. I drilled and drilled them, and they worked and worked, and they got better and they got steelier. It wasn't necessarily pretty, mind, and we didn't take any prisoners. Spike was always amongst it on the pitch and also off it: he took exception to the silly and sometimes brutal initiation ceremonies they had for new players at Newport and he stood up for himself.

That first season at Newport, though, was tough. We won only 18 of our 45 games, and another two in a tour of British Columbia. I suppose the highlight of that first season was reaching a Welsh Cup quarter-final, but Aberavon hammered us at home. Across the season we used 54 players. We needed consistency and discipline. As I always said, "Coaches are never happy," and I certainly wasn't happy with that first season.

I set about putting that extra bit of discipline into them, and it started to come together in my second season. We were up against it, mind. We'd lost Internationals Rob Ackerman and Gareth Evans to Cardiff and that was a blow, and we were unlucky with injuries too. I even had to play three times myself and I was into my forties by now. There were some dodgy decisions, too, especially when we lost to Swansea in the third round of the Welsh Cup.

But with former scrum half Allan 'Archie' Evans sat beside me on the bench, I watched us get off to a good start and, across the season, we won 31 from 54. Plus, we set club records for points (984) and tries (160). The downside was the loss of Colin Smart, who retired after being sent off in his 306th game for Newport.

Spike played in every game that season. He did all the pre-match team talks and he was my representative on the pitch. He was also involved in continuing hijinks off it. On one of our tours, after the players let the water out of the hotel swimming pool for a laugh, I had them marching like soldiers through the Portuguese resort where we were staying. Another time they got their own back by lacing my omelette with magic mushrooms. So, as you can see, while I'd brought a lot of discipline to their training and game, I didn't always keep them on the straight and narrow off it!

Spike was elected captain for 1983/84, and we brought in some more new boys, including lock Andrew Perry, hooker Hassan Ali and back row Andy Pocock; Glamorgan Wanderers full back Phil Steele and outside half Andy Phillips; and Bridgend centres Chris Williams and Robbie James.

Spike had managed to poach Phil Steele for us. Phil says he was a bit in awe of me when he joined:

I was a bit unsure of him and he hadn't spoken much to me, so I went up to him and thought I'd start a conversation about his training shoes. We all used to wear spikes in pre-season training for running up and down slopes. "They're nice trainers, Tony. Are they spikes?" I asked innocently. "No, they're not, College boy. They're mine," he said, and walked off.

Phil had been asked to join Cardiff, but says he came to Newport because they were much more welcoming. It was more like a family. I used to call him and Marc Batten the "College boys". They found training with me was different from being at Cardiff Met – the "college of knowledge", I called it.

This is what Phil remembers about it:

Tony was very, very regimented about training. At seven o'clock you started. If you weren't there, training started without you and he'd give you a bollocking when you turned up. He blew the whistle at seven and that was that. If you turned up at 7:01, you were late.

Training always started off with banks of two – Colin Smart and Rhys Morgan, the props, at the front, because they would set the pace – and it would be four laps. I think it was the same as what Prosser used to do at Pontypool.

Another thing he did used to confuse me. I'd come from college, where there was cutting-edge coaching. But one of Charlie's drills was to get us down on the goal-line and then make us commando crawl to the 22. Get up, sprint to the halfway line, then commando crawl again to the other 22, and then sprint to the end. Charlie would be shouting at us too: "Steeley, get your arse down, look, or it'll be shot off." And I'd be thinking, what has this got to do with me in a game?

Now, Charlie had been in the TA – he loved the army, so this was his thing. And commando crawling, that's what the SAS do. If you think you're fit, do that for 22 metres a couple of times and you'll think different. Of course all the forwards would lap it up. They loved it.

We used to train first of all at St Julian's School. Running up and down these steep banks. Charlie wouldn't say a word, just, "Ready? On the whistle," and then he'd blow and off we'd go.

In about August we started training at Rodney Parade. We'd be doing this unopposed rugby, all forward play, rolling maul, ruck, then a scrum. The backs wouldn't get a sniff of the ball.

After one session Charlie came up to me.

"What d'you think of the training, then, College?"

I said, "The forward play, Charlie, is brilliant, it's a science, but when do the backs get it?"

"About fucking April," he said, and walked off.

I saw a lot of good in the lads that year. That October, we beat Cardiff at Rodney Parade with wing Tim Harrison scoring a hat-trick, and enjoyed getting the better of Gloucester, Llanelli, Ebbw Vale, London Welsh and Bath, among others – plus a decent draw against the Barbarians. We beat the club record for points again – breaking 1,000 for the first time. Another 31 victories. On the way back from a win, I'd gather the boys around me on the bus and sing one of my favourites, 'Do Not Forsake Me, Oh My Darling', from the film *High Noon*.

Spike was playing great rugby and after every game I'd give him a lecture that he should only have a few drinks and behave. Every chance I got, I mentioned him to the WRU. He called me his "door-to-door canvasser"! I knew he was playing so well that sooner or later they'd have to forgive and forget. Eventually, they let him train with the Wales team and he had one foot in the door. I told him to keep his head down at training, work hard and keep his gob shut. Soon after, he got to captain the 'B' team in France – and won – and then made his debut in the 1984 Five Nations against Ireland. He became the first person in a hundred-odd years to captain Wales on his debut.

Before he headed off to Lansdowne Road, I told him that my lucky charm in Dublin was to feed the ducks in the park at St Stephen's Green before a game. He looked doubtful, but, apparently, after his breakfast at the Shelbourne, he nabbed some bread rolls and did what I suggested. The team beat Ireland 18-9.

Spike captained us again in 1984/85, and we had a good run, winning well over half our games, but we had a string of injuries and lost top try scorer Mike Lewis to a club in Italy.

I hated losing good players – committed players – but I enjoyed working with new ones. We brought in a future England International, full back Jon Callard; future Newport captain and Wales International Glenn George; former Wales scrum half Gerald Williams (from Bridgend); New Zealand-born centre Ross Knight; and full back Arwel Parry from Pontypool.

I really enjoyed nurturing young players. People like prop Alun 'Benny' Williams, who joined us that year. He remembers:

> I will never forget the day Charlie and Spikey came to my house in Bettws to ask my dad if I would like to play for Newport RFC. It was a dream come true for me. Then, at a time when I was struggling for fitness, he ran down from Malpas to my parents' house to take me out for a trundle. I was in the shower after a run, but I went out again with him: he pushed me hard! I will always be grateful to him for the effort he put in personally to make me a better player. That's a Lions and Wales legend coming down to ask me to go for a run with him. He was just passionate about wanting to get the best out of every player.
>
> Sometimes Charlie's training methods were unusual. At Monday training after a game we'd lost, when the backs had had a particular off-day despite the pack controlling affairs up front, Charlie decided the backs should get to know how hard it is to win the ball at scrum time. First, he had them on the scrum machine – and they did okay on that. But then he made them scrummage against the first team pack. There were a lot of moans and groans and sore necks, but it worked! The backs learned to respect possession and didn't give it too easily after that!

In 1985/86 we won the Snelling Sevens for the first time since 1967. In the League, we did alright again but we got embroiled in the kind of controversy I knew from Pontypool. We were playing at Bristol and it was a right old to-do. The referee didn't like it and he walked off the field, complaining that the match had descended into "street violence". A few weeks later we had three players sent off at Old Deer Park against my old Pontypool foes, London Welsh.

But we were playing some great rugby and they couldn't ignore us. We beat Swansea and Aberavon to reach the Cup Final against Cardiff in April 1986. The atmosphere at the National Stadium was electric and, while I tried to stay calm, I really wanted this victory. Spike wanted it too, but I knew I needed to keep him cool if we were to have half a chance. I gave him a few of my talks but once he was out there, there was nothing I could do. He butted his old rival Alan Phillips in the first scrum. All the same, we pushed them hard, right up to the whistle, losing 28–21. It was one of the great Cup finals. That season we also took 4th place in the Merit Table and 5th place in the Welsh Unofficial Championship.

But injury came back to haunt us in 1986/87. After a cracking start, we lost seven players to injury against Neath and were just too weak to put up much of a battle in the rest of the first half of the season. But I kept the boys training hard and worked the casualties back into the team as they started to regain fitness. After Christmas, team strength restored, we went on a hell of a run, winning 22 out of 23, including a first win at Aberavon in 15 years, a first at Bristol for 10 years and recorded major wins over Newbridge (52-0) and Pontypool (43-3).

The downside was the Welsh Cup, where we went down to a quarter-final defeat at Cardiff. It was a miserable day. We'd dreamt of getting our own back for the final defeat the previous season and Marc Batten scored a fine try for us early on. But we were refused a penalty try for Cardiff collapsing the scrum at least three times in the last few minutes and we had what we thought was a try by John Widdecombe ruled out by the ref. Although we'd led for much of the match, my mate Mark Ring had put Cardiff ahead and we went out.

Despite that, this was the season we battered all our previous records. A points total of 1,286. Most wins: 39. Most tries: 198. But we still just missed out on a title. We were runners-up in both the Merit Table and the Welsh Unofficial

Championship. Spike played his 200th game that season for Newport – sorry, Charlie Faulkner RFC.

I should have moved on then.

Spike decided not to stand for captaincy for the following season (1987/88) and after getting sent off against Newbridge, he decided he'd had enough. It was a sign of trouble to come. Like Pross at Pontypool, I'd built the team around the pack. Unfortunately, within weeks of the season beginning, we'd lost Frank Hillman, Wayne Rendall, John Widdecombe and Andrew Perry to injury. Then we lost Robert 'Bosun' Young and Alun Williams to suspension. Alun remembers:

> When 'Bosun' and myself were suspended, the Newport committee doubled our WRU suspensions! It was an attempt to make players more disciplined. I know Spike and Charlie fought hard against this. We played hard, we intimidated packs, and these decisions didn't support what Charlie and Spike were trying to achieve.

I felt it was time to move on.

On 21 November 1987, after a win at Llandovery, I announced I was stepping down. My co-coach Roy Duggan and acting captain Roger Powell resigned as well.

I felt pretty happy with my seasons at Newport. We'd gone from being one of the worst teams in the Championship to one of the best. But I'll leave the final judgement up to Bobby, who was always somewhere in the background, always supportive:

> He did a fucking great job at Newport. He talked sense, was a great coach, knew the game. He could see what had gone wrong and could tell the players from his own experience how to put it right.

Chapter Thirteen

A hero with Charlie's Angels

In 1989 I started on a rugby adventure which began in farce and ended with me being hailed a real-life hero.

To begin, in case you haven't heard of them, let me tell you about the Maccabiah Games. The best way to describe them is how they are sometimes nicknamed: the Jewish Olympics. Every four years, in the year following the Olympic Games, Jewish athletes from around the world head to Israel to take part in all sorts of sports. The games include a competition for Jewish rugby players.

That year, I was sitting in the press room with Bobby and Graham in Cardiff after the Schweppes Cup Final when I was approached by a writer named Gerry Greenberg. Gerry was going to be managing the Great Britain team in Israel. He asked me if I'd be interested in coaching the rugby team, which was going to the Games for the first time.

I said yes immediately. I've never been able to resist anything to do with rugby and coaching was always the second-best thing to playing, but it wasn't just that: Israel was one of those places that I really wanted to see, especially Jerusalem. I was fascinated by its history and culture and its meaning to so many people.

To be honest, I didn't know too much about what I was letting myself in for – I'm not Jewish and I confess, I'd never heard of the Games – but it was rugby and so I loved it.

Anyway, it wasn't a wealthy affair and we basically had to fundraise to pay our way. I asked my old mate Spike Watkins to come to an event in London where people would pay to hear us say a few words. The more celebs we had the better.

We did our routine and it went well, but then I found out they hadn't booked us a hotel. Unfortunately, we made a bad decision. Spike decided to drive home and set off carefully down the M4. At some point Spike saw the blue lights of a police Range Rover in his mirrors and he accelerated. They caught up with us at the Severn Bridge. Spike was just over the limit and got a year ban. Hence the farce mentioned at the start of the chapter.

I was to train a 26-player British squad, with players from all over – from Brighton to Glasgow. There were three or four players from Wales, but the majority were from London – old boys' outfits like Merchant Taylors, Bealonians, Bancroft and Old Millhillians. Many of these were a different breed to what I was used to. The London players weren't rugby players in the south Wales sense. What we thought was an easy game, they thought was a dirty game.

There was only a handful of first-class players in the squad, including Ian Marcus of Nuneaton, Paul Balcombe of Wasps and Richard Gordon of Roundhay. I could see there was a lot to do with the whole squad with regard to fitness and skills – and we didn't have much time. I had about six or eight weeks to get them ready.

We trained at the Bancroft Rugby Club at Buckhurst Hill in Essex, and I'd travel up with Dai Lubin in his Astra van every Sunday morning. Dai played for Glamorgan Wanderers and was going to play loosehead for me in the GB team. Dai remembers it better than me:

To be honest, Charlie just coached forwards. To the backs, he'd say, "You boys go up the field and kick the ball!" His passion was the scrum. He was a knowledgeable coach,

Charlie – tough as can be on the pitch, lovely off it. In training, it was a case of "Do as I say, or else!"

Charlie saw what he had and went to work. Everything was about getting us fit, fit, fit. He trained the bollocks off us!

What I did find, though, was that what they lacked in experience and finesse, they certainly made up for with enthusiasm. The Maccabiah games were a big deal for them. It meant a lot.

Through hard training, we forged a bond very quickly. They were really great boys. By the time we were ready to leave for Israel, they were referring to themselves as "Charlie's Angels".

We hired a minibus from south Wales with supporters and some parents, and met up with the whole GB team at the airport. Right from the off, we got on the wrong side of the some of the other athletes. I'll let Dai Lubin explain:

Under Charlie's guidance, we were immediately vilified because we started drinking at the airport and didn't stop till we landed in Israel. We were outcasts. We went on to drink and sing our way around Israel and Charlie was with us every step of the way.

When I got to Israel, I realised how big the whole thing was. More than 4,000 athletes from 46 countries, from India to Spain, Argentina to Yugoslavia. There was karate, weightlifting, swimming, tennis: all the sports – you name it. Rugby's not really a centrepiece, but GB wanted to give it a go.

We were based in Netanya in a place which was half-college, half-army camp. There was a bar downstairs and I got chatting to someone there. His name was Shimon and he'd been one of the leaders in the 1976 raid on Entebbe, a rescue mission launched by Israeli commandos to free hostages taken when terrorists hijacked an Air France plane and diverted it to Uganda. He was now head of security for the camp. We went off together into Netanya for more drinks, in his battered old Datsun filled with weapons. There was a machine gun under the seat and a pistol in the glove compartment. I've always loved the military since my days in the TA and Shimon and I became the best of friends, with most of our chat being about weapons, much to the amusement of my team. Dai Lubin remembers:

> On the last night, we had these massive celebrations and we all got back into the camp in the early hours – daybreak virtually – and all of a sudden we could hear shooting and machine guns from the rifle range. We didn't know what the heck was going on. And then Charlie turns up with a broad smile on his face, wearing an Israeli uniform. Shimon had taken him down the shooting range!

The boys laughed because I'd had to wear the Israeli Army uniform, or I wouldn't have been let in.

I'd said to Shimon, "What do I say if anyone says anything to me?"

"Just say 'Shalom'," Shimon told me.

So I wandered through the army camp, saying, "Shalom, butt!"

Despite the high spirits, we didn't ignore training – just the opposite. Because it was so hot, the matches weren't going to start until nine at night, but I had the boys training in the midday sun. One of our second rows collapsed one day and we laid him out in the shade of a tree.

The main thing you noticed about the Games – and the whole country, to be honest – was the security. I'd played once at Ballymena in Northern Ireland on a pitch surrounded by troops, but this was worse, in the sense that the threat seemed to be everywhere. There were more armed police and soldiers at the opening ceremony than I've ever seen in one place. And all the while, specialist police and sniffer dogs were sweeping the stadium – at Ramat Gan near Tel Aviv – for bombs. And it was going to be like this for the whole 11 days of competition. At some point we heard about a terror attack on a bus, which killed 14 people. There was a lot of fear and tension, which we weren't used to. But we were here for the Games and we had to concentrate on our rugby.

It was a round-robin tournament and our first match was against a 'Rest of the World' team, which was packed with top-class South Africans starved of international opposition because of the international sporting boycott in protest at Apartheid. It was a rough one, as we'd had a big argument with them in the mess hall on the first morning there. The Military Police had had to break us up. There were fists in the mess and on the pitch. I took this to heart and, when I thought our boys weren't playing well enough, I raced along the touchline telling them to sort it out. To be fair, they did. I was proud of them. But we were well beaten, 17-3, mainly due to the kicking of their outside half, Anton Chait.

We now had to win three games in five days. I put the boys through their paces and they responded tremendously. We beat Canada 25-10, with Brighton No. 8 Peter Noble scoring two fine tries and Balcombe adding a third. Scrum half Balcombe played brilliantly in the next game too, against the American Eagles, whose pack was big and hard. His clever kicks made sure the Eagles were always on the defensive. We hammered them – 23-3.

But we still needed to beat Israel to reach the final. And we had problems – a slew of injuries from the pack, including Richard Glynn, a former Oxford Blue.

Israel was a proper side – it was their International team we'd be facing, and they'd just gained valuable experience in France in a World Cup qualifying tournament. In the end, it wasn't pretty. It turned into a bit of a stalemate, which would be settled by the boot. Our skipper, Ian Marcus, won it for us. In fact, across the five games he kicked 52 points for us. He, like many of the boys, played five games in eight days in exhausting heat.

And so we met that 'Rest of the World' team again in the final. We played well and scored a push-over try against a much bigger South African pack. But the game was lost and we left with a silver medal. Charlie's Angels had flown, but not quite reached the heavens.

Dai Lubin said:

The push-over try against that huge pack actually made it feel like a victory. In just a few weeks, Charlie had moulded us into the best pack out there.

It would have been great to win gold, and it was within our sights, but silver was pretty good. All in all, a great trip. Some fine rugby, and I got to see a fascinating country, its military history and culture, and visit Yad Vashem, Israel's official memorial to the victims of the Holocaust. That was an honour.

Unexpectedly, though, it wouldn't be the matches I'd be remembered for at those Games.

The Games ended with a closing ceremony that started with a long march through Jerusalem and then into the stadium, which was absolutely packed – just like a stadium would be for a Commonwealth or Olympic Games.

It was what happened to me after the athletes and supporters came back out into the streets afterwards that a written history of the Maccabiah Games would call "arguably the most impressive performance of the Games".

This was a strange one. The streets around the Wailing Wall in Jerusalem were packed for the final celebrations. All the athletes were there, all waving their flags, marching through with huge smiles on their faces. Everywhere you looked, there were people. And then suddenly there was a bang, smoke and screams. Everyone assumed it was a bomb going off. Fear was so high, with everyone having been tense before it even happened. The whole crowd began to run away from the growing cloud of smoke – it was like a stampede.

I started to run too, and right in the middle of the charging crowds I saw a pushchair. I thought it must be empty, abandoned by a parent who'd picked up their child and fled. But as I got close, I could see there was a young child in it. Just a toddler. I couldn't believe it. It must have got separated from its mum or dad. The crowds were rushing past, and the pushchair got knocked and tipped over. I dashed over, made sure the little child was secure and lifted it up. I held the chair above my head and started to jog to the exit, careful not to miss my step. Some people saw me and let me through; others were just panicking, trying to rush past. Smoke was filling the air now, and my eyes were streaming. People were coughing, being sick from the smoke, crying. I was pretty frightened myself, to be honest, but I knew that if I didn't get the child out of there, it would be trampled.

When I got to safety, I found a police officer and he found the mum. The police told the press later that I had saved the child's life and it became a huge thing, a big fuss. Investigators found out that the stampede itself was caused by a smoke bomb, not explosives, but that didn't stop the danger – quite a few people were trampled and hurt. That poor little mite could have been among them.

But I only did what I had to do. I think lots of people would have done it. I was just there, in the right place and at the right time to do the right thing.

I'd got separated from the team – they'd gone on ahead. They were waiting on the bus and didn't know a thing about what had happened. But when I stepped on the bus, my eyes were still stinging so much from the smoke that it looked as if I'd been weeping, so I had to tell them everything.

I've forgotten a lot over the years, but I always remember this: that little child did not cry once, despite everything going on all around them.

Chapter Fourteen

"Show a bit of commitment!"

IN THE 1992/93 season I headed to Cardiff RFC to assist coach organiser Alexander 'Alec' Evans, brought in from Australia after the club had had one of the worst runs in its history.

A successful club can get complacent, rest on its laurels, and assume things are always going to go well. Cardiff had discovered that wasn't the case, and only avoided relegation at the end of the 1991/92 season because the WRU decided to switch to a 12-team Premiership. For the next season, Cardiff brought a coaching team in to go right back to the basics. That's the way I always approached things for the packs I coached. I saw myself as a scrum doctor, I suppose, taking players back to the simple principles of scrummaging and to my mantra of practise, practise, practise...

Alec brought an excitement to training which we all found inspiring. People enjoyed coming along to see our training sessions. Again, I concentrated on – or obsessed over – discipline. One night the boys were out doing press-ups. I watched one for a while and then wandered over to him.

"What school did you go to?" I asked.

He told me.

"Did they teach you mathematics?"

"Yeah."

"Then can you tell me why you're doing 15 press-ups when I asked for 20?"

I took my old mate Spike for a one-to-one training session too, because he was getting into coaching. We met at Tredegar Park outside Newport and I'd brought balls and contact tackle-pads.

I gave Spike one of the tackle-pads but we were a man short. A guy came by, walking his dog, and we persuaded him to stand in. He was, shall we say, not built for the pack.

I charged at Spike, off-loading the ball before I hit him, then carried on and, getting carried away, took the man out.

The last thing I saw was the fear in the dog-walker's eyes.

According to Spike, I leaned over the poor guy and said, "Hey, butt, if you're going to do this properly, show a bit of commitment!"

Our coaching team at Cardiff included Terry Holmes, former Wales centre Alun Donovan and Malcolm Childs. We were later joined by Ian Bremner, Gwynne Griffiths and Steve Davies. We worked hard to get the confidence back in the players and we succeeded. They knew Alec had done great stuff on the coaching staff for Australia and obviously knew all about my career and Terry's.

In our first season, we got the club back on track. New winger Nigel Walker came in on good form and became a favourite with the fans, and we started the season with five straight wins and a very narrow defeat at Llanelli.

Soon after, we beat my old friends at Pontypool and then overcame Swansea with a last-minute try from Steve Ford. It was the first full house in years that day, and I can still remember the roar when Steve went over. Such was the thrill of beating our rivals that the supporters lined the tunnel under the stand to applaud our boys off. If that kind of thing doesn't build confidence in a player, nothing will.

It didn't all quite go to plan. I know fans still remember how we left the SWALEC Cup that year: defeat at home to Fourth Division St Peter's (who I also coached for a while later on). That was a very hard pill to swallow. But learning the right lessons from defeat is important too. It's something coaches have to instil in players, that. It's also a familiar Cup story: never underestimate the opposition if they come from the lower leagues.

We remained strong in the League, though, especially in important matches against Pontypridd and Bath. Defeat at Bridgend – a game we were winning – robbed us of the League title. If we'd won that, we'd have done it, I reckon, because we went on to beat Newport and Swansea. We finished runners-up to Llanelli. Quite a few of our boys got capped for Wales that year, including Nigel Walker, Mike Rayer, prop Mike Griffiths, our captain Mike Hall and Simon Hill.

That summer the club went on a memorable three-week tour of Australia. Some felt it was too much; that it would exhaust the players ahead of the new season. But I think it did the opposite: it brought the squad together, improved their performance and showed them a bit of the excitement of what being at a top club could be like. We beat a very strong Cairns Barbarians XV – which featured several All Blacks – and got to visit the Great Barrier Reef, which was an off-field highlight. I believe it all inspired the boys.

We certainly started the 1993/94 season well again, although we ran out of steam at times. Over the season we scored more tries than anyone else and conceded fewer. We showed our strength by playing some of our best rugby in the second half: this went back to my own experiences at Pontypool, and maintaining fitness to such levels that when the opposition faltered, you carried on. I learnt that from Pross, and it's a mantra repeated by top coaches in all sports.

But the highlight of the year was that we kicked out any of the bad feeling left over from the embarrassment of the defeat by St Peter's. We went right through the Cup this time, facing down Llanelli in the final and beating them 15-8. Our boys were again picked for Wales, including Adrian Davies and Hemi Taylor, and they helped us win the Five Nations.

Winning the Cup was a great feeling but it's League success that shows a club's consistency over a season. It had eluded us so far but there was a great feeling at our 1994 pre-season training in the Jersey sunshine – where we all got to meet Ian Woosnam, the first Welshman to win one of Golf's Majors when he claimed the 1991 Masters at Augusta. We took a sense of belief right into the 1994/95 season with us and by Christmas we were top of the League, and we stayed strong to win the title. We also got named Whitbread British Team of the Year. Good fellas, Whitbread!

We failed to recapture the Cup, though – knocked out by a very good Swansea side – but all in all a good year for the club and new Chief Executive Gareth Davies.

The 1995 Rugby World Cup was not a memorable one for Wales, but we had Alec coaching, Mike Hall as captain and ten other players in the squad that went to South Africa.

Rugby was changing. A European competition was coming and, bigger still, the game was "going professional". For generations, players had given their all just for the sport. It was fine. It was sport. We loved it. But it had also meant that, as the game developed during my own career, players had to make decisions about their rugby lives and about who they would play for based on what kind of job they could get to support their family. It's hard to believe now for younger sports fans that we could be at the top of our sport but still working five days a week to earn a living.

More immediately for us at Cardiff, Alec left halfway through the 1995/96 season and Terry took over as head coach. Hemi became our skipper, while our boy Jonathan Humphreys captained Wales. We had some cracking games, including a one-point defeat of touring team Fiji in front of a packed crowd.

In the first ever Heineken Cup we took on Bègles-Bordeaux in the rain of south-western France, which made those of us who'd suffered a Valleys downpour feel very much at home.

It was a cracking game, played in an atmosphere which felt like an International, and we got a draw. When we hammered Ulster in the next match, that put us through to the semis against Leinster, to be played in Dublin. In Ireland, we faced howling gales, which had swept across the country and into Wales, grounding a plane of club officials in Cardiff. Tries from Mike Hall and Hemi Taylor, and the boot of Adrian Davies, helped earn us a 23-14 victory and we began to believe we might win be the first winners of the new tournament. The final was to be played in Cardiff: a good omen, a boost – or just added pressure?

It was to be a nail-biter. Toulouse had us on the back foot at the start, but Adrian Davies kept us in it. We were three points down as the clock passed the eighty, when we got a penalty and Davies scored again – he had a dream day with the boot.

Extra time and another penalty each, before we got penalised for hands in a ruck. Our loosehead Andy Lewis denied he'd done anything wrong and we – and the twenty-plus thousand Cardiff fans – bloody well agreed, but the penalty was just 18 metres out. Unmissable. A sitter for Christophe Deylaud, although Mark Ring tried to put him off: "The closer ones are always the harder ones," Ringo shouted at him.

Nevertheless, Deylaud slotted over and we lost 21-18. That first European Cup was filled with good experiences but that was a desperately disappointing end. We were almost there... although to be fair, they played really well, and we probably lost it in that opening ten minutes when we let them have the run of the game.

The League that year should have given us comfort. We scored the most points and the most tries, and Steve Ford crossed the line more times than anyone in Heineken League history. But, somehow, we didn't win. It was down to another change in the game: the try bonus-point system. That meant we won the most games but still lost! Two defeats by Bridgend and another by Newport did for us. We came second.

Loads more boys came through for Wales, prop Lyndon Mustoe among them. But professionalism and the promise of lucrative contracts elsewhere meant we lost some decent players, including Adrian Davies and Ringo. To make up, we brought a lot of boys in for 1996/97, including Dai Young and Rob Howley (soon both to tour with the Lions).

I was gutted to lose Mustoe from the front row in a pre-season match at Leicester. A bad omen which gave us a bad start to the season. We felt a bit like a new team with all the changes, and then had boys heading off to International training, which shook us up further. Towards the end of the season, Alec Evans came back as rugby director to oversee the coaches again, but by then we'd steadied the ship, getting fourth place in the League when at one point we'd looked much further out of it.

It was another good Cup year for us. Howley's try and Jonathan Davies' drop goal sealed a 26-24 win at Wasps in the Heineken Cup, and, although we lost to Toulouse, we beat Munster and Milan and qualified for the quarter finals. Walker scored a great solo try at home to Bath and we flew to Brive in France for the semis. Snow and ice made the journey difficult, and then a sending off on the pitch put the game beyond us. We went out, but it was a pretty good run to get to the semis against such strong opposition.

But we went a step better in the SWALEC Cup, reaching the final against Swansea and beating them 33-26 in what was to be the last match played at the National Stadium – the Arms Park, as everyone called it. Hemi recovered from an injury to captain us that day.

That was the last of the good times, I think. I stayed on for a couple more seasons, but no more silverware.

Overall, they were good years at Cardiff. Good years, and great fans. We were let go in 1999, at another time of great change for rugby in Cardiff and Wales. Mike Hall retired and Gareth Davies left Cardiff after twelve years as player and five as chief executive. And, just next door, the Millennium Stadium was opening for the Rugby World Cup and a new generation of players.

For me, after decades of involvement with the game, it was a time to look back on a life in rugby well-spent.

Chapter Fifteen

Playing to the final whistle

How do you begin to compare rugby in Wales in the era in which I played to what it has become since? It's a big question, and one asked of players from any golden era of the past.

There are a lot of things that are better about the game of today than the sport in my day. Players properly paid and compensated, facilities better, wives treated more respectfully by the game's authorities, for a start.

But there's a lot that's worse too.

At the last International I went to, everyone was drunk around me, the fans were booing the opposition, tackles resulted in cries of "Off! Off! Off!" It was like a football match. When the Australian kicker was taking a kick, I could see people shining torches from their phones to put him off. I didn't enjoy it.

The world's changed, of course, and you have to accept that, and I don't want to criticise anyone. But for rugby communities in Wales in my era, rugby was a religion. And that stemmed from the fact that the club game really mattered. The club was part of the community. It made the community proud. Sometimes it was almost all the community had, all it had to be proud of.

When we took the pitch, we were representing them. The faces in the crowd. Our win was their win, their pride. The fans who watched us knew us, saw us in the street or at work; we were part of the community, and, if we lost, we'd get some stick from them in person.

When me and the other Gwent boys would meet up with the Wales squad, we'd hear everyone going on about the Scarlets and the Jacks and that incredible local derby, but we'd say to Grav and Phil Bennett, "Look, where we are, there's several top first team sides within 25 miles of each other: Pontypool, Cross Keys, Ebbw Vale, Tredegar, Abertillery..." Our local derbies weren't one or two games a year – we had them all the time.

As Pross himself is quoted as saying in *The Good, The Bad and the Ugly* by Nick Bishop and Alun Carter, "People would come to watch Pontypool play Abertillery or Cross Keys rather than watch Wales playing the Springboks!"

And let me add to that: there wasn't a single bad front row in any of those derby games we had to play. We lived by a code to survive. Train, practise, train, practise. And we'd always remember the eleventh commandment: "Thou shalt not get caught." After all, winning was important.

Phil Steele remembers a story from my coaching days with Newport:

I remember one day we lost to Newbridge at home and that was a big derby. It was a terrible night, terrible weather. Paul Turner dropped for goal for Newbridge and I was the full back right under the bar, and I could see the ball went over and so I instinctively raised my hand to show he'd scored. You see, I'd seen Mike Gibson do it when Barry John dropped a goal for Wales and I thought, if it's good enough for one of the great players of all time then it's good enough for me. After the game, the chairman of the Newport supporters club came up to me and said, "That was fabulous – an example of real sportsmanship, which reflects well on the club." Charlie saw it differently! He gave me the biggest bollocking. "You don't give them fuck all, Steeley! Fuck all!"

We became hard because we had to play hard. There is nothing stronger than a local rivalry, than a rivalry with a town or village five miles over the hill which is just like yours – except that *it's not*.

We had that toughness in our hearts, and that sense that we were the club and the club was the community. But professionalism changed the way players were viewed and then the regions broke down the rivalries and changed the game in Wales.

Did it also remove some of the hunger? Our sense of community meant that we were always hungry. Winning always mattered. We didn't know how to give anything less than everything. Eddie Butler told a story to Nick Bishop and Alun Carter about how he brought a young Cambridge University team down to Pontypool. It was early in the season and Butler wanted to widen the students' experience. Pross pulled me and the others aside before the game and told us the opposition were just kids out to learn, and we should go easy on them. Eddie says he heard Pross say, "Whatever you do, don't touch them – no booting or punching!" Unfortunately, their flanker spent much of the game getting on the wrong side of the ruck and killing the ball. I let it go most of the game, but close to the end I'd had enough and gave him a 'physical' telling off. He left the field with blood pouring out of the top of his head. Pross wasn't happy and I had to try to apologise, but their guy played his game, and learned a lesson. For me, the opposition was the opposition, I suppose. 80 minutes is a long time not to touch someone in a game which is so completely physical.

We worked all week, trained Mondays and Thursdays, and played rugby Saturday, Wednesday, Saturday, Wednesday, in the wind and the rain, and we loved it. And we didn't have water breaks! At Pontypool, Pross wouldn't even let us have an orange at half-time. "Hungry lions hunt the best!" he said.

So, yes: we were hungry, we had the skills – running and handling – power and technique, but we also had an iron resolve.

Our hardness showed itself in the scrum. The scrum is about struggle and strength. It's about determination and planting your feet. *We ain't moving.* The way we saw it, if you have a team in which the scrum's not going to go backwards, then you are halfway to winning that match, because it's all about having that scrum right. That was the Pross philosophy, the Pontypool philosophy and my philosophy.

And you've seen it even in modern rugby: if the scrum's in trouble, the team is. Think about what South Africa did against Wales in 2021. Well, in some ways you could look at Bobby, Graham and me and say what we did was very similar to that South African front row. When you're doing damage like that, that's when the team gets on top. The Wales scrum of 2021, well, every time they put the ball in, they gave away a penalty. They even struggled a bit against Fiji.

It's obvious to you by now, I know, that I'm passionate about good forward play. To be honest, before the Pontypool Front Row was honed under Pross, I'd watch good players, big fellas, who just couldn't scrummage. They couldn't go low like I did with a straight back. I did everything to build my technique and learn all the secrets of the scrum. I still give my tips whenever anyone asks. As you're kindly reading my book, I'll tell you.

Life's good when you've got a good hooker alongside you, binding, but you must remember to bind on the opposition as well. Every loosehead needs to get his feet inside the tighthead and always engage off two feet, rather than just the left foot. You get more power that way.

And when you're under pressure, don't lift your feet. That's the worst thing you can do. You need to anchor your feet, plant them in the turf, drop your knees and ride the pressure out. That's what gives you the will and the pride not to go backwards.

I played both tighthead and loosehead, and it's become fashionable over the years to see the tighthead role as the harder position. I don't agree: tighthead is tougher when the player's protecting his own ball, but when your pack is attacking the opposition put-in, then the tighthead has the big advantage of having two shoulders bound into the scrum; the loosehead has just one.

Technical, I know, but important to someone who's studying the scrum. And the scrum is about technique and strength. Now, today, a lot of props don't realise all that, but I learned it the hard way.

After every game for Cross Keys in the early years of my career, I grabbed hold of someone from the opposition front row – people like Gordon Ship – and asked them for their advice. None of them ever pushed me away or said, "You're the opposition, we're not telling you, that's a secret!" The props would always be open with another. And it was great, and I learnt a lot.

Over the years we've been asked to comment on a lot by the press – including Pontypool's woes, financial and on-field – but most often we're asked about the Wales team of the day, the arrival of Garin Jenkins as the first decent scrummaging hooker in yonks, some of our performances over the years when it was hard to remember the good times.

But after I finished playing there was no continuity with the players. I coached the under-21 team for Wales but never heard anything from the 'A' team. No one ever came looking for our knowledge. The laws had changed: yes, we understood that. They'd stopped the pulling down of the tighthead by the loosehead. They'd changed some things which removed physical challenges from the scrum. They'd introduced some safety where once the law of the jungle ruled. Fine!

But the basics of scrummaging remained the same. They could have come to us for advice. But I was never asked; Pricey was never asked; Bobby was never asked. We were never asked for advice or thoughts. They must have forgotten me – and the Pontypool Front Row!

*

I did get one unexpected call from a Wales team, though. I was asked to coach the forwards for the Wales women's team, and that turned out to be an honour. The team had had a real thrashing against England in 1996 at Leicester Tigers' Welford Road ground and so I went in to give head coach Paul Ringer a hand.

Lisa Walsh, who was playing back then as Lisa Jones, remembers:

> We were struggling in the scrum, being pushed backwards at a rate of knots, losing 56-3 that day.
>
> Charlie joined us at our Wales camps in Sophia Gardens the following year, helping Paul Ringer take care of the forwards. Charlie was hugely popular with the girls right from the start. So kind, funny and knowledgeable in all things rugby – especially the scrum!
>
> I can still hear him shouting, "Squeeze, knees, drive": squeeze the binding, flex the knees and then drive on the engage. A great drill for getting the timing right and one that paid off the following year when Wales played England, losing by just two points, 22-24, and beat Scotland 10-0 and Ireland 32-5.

We trained hard but had a lot of fun with that squad. I had fun, too, coaching at Caerphilly and St Peter's.

*

I played for Wales over four seasons and we won the Championship on each occasion. I had three Triple Crowns and two Grand Slams. That's a short International career but packed with silverware, as they say. I'm proud of that. I was lucky to be in such a fine team – a team of legends. And it was us, as Graham says, who "provided the foundation for the gifted backs like Gareth, Benny, Gerald, JPR and others to strut their brilliance".

The Pontypool Front Row has become almost a myth – although, by God, anyone who played against us knew we were real enough.

And it was Ray Prosser who made us, who made me. He's the shining light that hangs over my career and I can't sum up what's happened to me, and what it's all meant, without focusing on Pross. He coached me and he guided me. It was him that got me to a place where I could play for Wales and the Lions. The same goes for Graham and Bobby. From that first game we played together in September 1973, he worked hard to turn us into one of the finest units in sport.

I'll be forever grateful to that man for what he did for me. He was also my inspiration when I went into coaching myself. Naturally, in 2005 when Graham, Bobby and I came together to be inducted into the Welsh Rugby Hall of Fame, we made sure Pross was there too.

And when Pross died in November 2019, the Pontypool Front Row stood together in the church and, right at the end of the service, as the curtains came round and the coffin went off, we all sang Max Boyce's song. It was so sad but marvellous at the same time. We were all cut up. I was on the verge of breaking down, but I never did. I held on, but there were tears filling my eyes.

For me, Pross was the best coach of all and we were very lucky to play under him. He trained us to play not for 80 minutes but for 90 minutes. And that's why we were successful. Nine times out of ten, the opposition had had it in the last 20 minutes but we kept at it and at it, and that's where we won a lot of games.

Pross never gave in either. Long after we and he had all left the club, he had carried on walking up the grotto hill above Pontypool Park.

*

Over the years the lasting fame of the Pontypool Front Row has occasionally rung on my doorbell. At one point an image of the PFR was printed on a very smart T-shirt to raise funds for Pontypool. In 1991, we and a pile of other Welsh players appeared in a film called *Old Scores* with Glyn Houston and Windsor Davies. It was about a linesman who confessed on his deathbed to making a mistake in a Wales-New Zealand game. Decades on, the old players have to replay the match. It was fun. We were all back on the pitch together! And also in the 1990s, for some reason, Graham, Bobby and I ended up dancing on *The Mike Doyle Show* as he sang 'Hip To Be Square'. Someone posted the clip on Facebook. It's quite good dancing! But, probably fortunately, I've forgotten everything about the experience.

As the years passed, we've continued to have our plaudits.

In November 1999, looking back over a century of Welsh rugby, top writer Paul Rees picked his dream XV and said the Pontypool Front Row "deserve inclusion as a trio".

He continued, "Totally different individuals, they complemented each other and made the leap from club to International rugby effortlessly." A lovely compliment.

And my old buddy Spike Watkins picked me for his all-time best World XV, alongside Robert Paparemborde, Terry Holmes, Phil Bennett, David Campese, Gerald Davies and Serge Blanco. Spike also picked his dirtiest XV – he included himself but kindly left me out!

And it's the judgement of friends that means the most. As Noel Williams says:

It's funny looking back at the Pontypool Front Row. They were all hard players and Charlie didn't take any prisoners, that's the best way to put it. Any prop that played against Charlie, Charlie would just want to best him; whoever it was, Charlie would be the boss and that's it. But he is gentle in many ways. Graham is exactly the same. Off the field, they're really nice people. On the field, they had a job to do and they did their job.

Looking back, Charlie is one of the characters of rugby. But he's like two different people: you've got that man who's a gentleman – nice, quiet with a lovely laugh. And then you've got that man who was on the field. I wouldn't have liked to be facing him, to be honest, and I don't think many others wanted to!

And Bobby says:

When you're with Charlie you're fighting like fuck, you know, but you've got a man on your side who'll stick right there with you and give you a bit of safety.

When you're playing, they can be saying, "You're the best in Wales" or "the best in the world", but you'll always meet somebody who's going to be equal to you. Now, I played with Charlie and I'll tell you straight: nobody ever beat Charlie. We had players that matched us, where we had to work really hard, but nobody ever beat him. Charlie was never bettered, but he bettered a lot of other people.

He would sky some boys in that scrum. Fucking hell. He was a strong, strong-willed man when he played.

Thanks, Bobby. Bobby's been a special person in my life. We came through from the bottom to the top. We did our bit. All the way from Whitehead's, where we both worked for years and played together, to Sarries, Cross Keys and Pontypool. There we met Graham, of course. Three became one then, to some extent. On the field, we were the Pontypool Front Row, just us three – no one else could have replaced any one of us. The Viet Gwent.

There were others who helped me too. I'd like to mention John Dawes and Ray Williams, the coaching organiser at Wales, for all they did for me. It was fitting that it was Ray who shouted across the training ground to tell me I was flying out to be with the Lions. He was almost as happy as me.

Away from rugby, there's my wonderful wife Jill, of course. She's stood by me throughout. Helped me in my life and career. We have three children and six lovely grandchildren. I love them all. Some of my happiest times have been our holidays together in Spain, often not just in the company of the family but also old rugby mates like John Blackborow and Paddy Burke.

My biggest disappointment? Okay, you know this: it is without doubt that defeat against New Zealand in 1978 when Haden jumped out of the line.

But I've something to add.

Some years later, still smarting with a bit of anger, I met Haden at a function following a World Rugby Classic tournament in Bermuda.

When we sat together at a table for dinner, I asked him to "dive across the table and pass the salt"!

That really made me laugh. Made me feel a bit better!

*

Over the years, of course, there was a lot of talk about my age. It became a big thing, even when I was playing great and it obviously didn't matter. It was just a number. I treated a lot of it as a joke. The Welsh boys spent the first few seasons ribbing me about it. "When were you born?" "How old are you then, Charlie?" I told them I was old enough, and not to worry.

Pricey says that when I got picked for Wales, a newspaper sent a reporter out searching for birth records of Newport Faulkners. The only problem was, he searched for 'Charlie' and not 'Anthony George'.

The thing to remember is that when Pricey scored his try in Paris I was right up there with him. He was 23. I was rapidly heading for my 34th birthday. It's not how old you are – it's who you play with, how hard you train, how much you want it.

All sports change, rugby as much as any other. I was a player of my time. I learnt my trade the hard way: working in front of a blazing furnace in a steelworks and playing in the rain and mud of a Valleys pitch. It was a tough life. No quarter given. But it's where I learnt the art of the scrummage and the philosophy the Pontypool Front Row lived or died on: "Never take a step back!"

I've tried to tell this story honestly. I like to talk about good things and good memories, not bad. So many things have happened, so many memories, but as George Thomas, my skipper when I played at the Sarries, says to me: "We've got lots of good stories about things we've done over the years, but I can't repeat any of them!"

It's been a wonderful life, playing and coaching in a sport I love. I admired and respected even my most vicious and brutal opponents.

And I hope they respected me.

Charlie's favourite players

NOT EXACTLY MY top team, just some of the players I've enjoyed playing with or against over the years.

Mervyn Davies
A good player and a great captain. Courageous and smart. I saw him take control of us in that debut game in Paris and always admired him.

Gareth Edwards
He had everything, didn't he? What can you say? An athlete, a sportsman, the epitome of skill and flair. Plus, I think I owe him for putting a word in with the selectors and getting me a chance to play for Wales at the age I was.

J J Williams
He had a terrific Lions tour in 1974. But I played with him all through my International career and he was a wonderful player – a really great player and a great man. You couldn't fault him, in my opinion. He could pass, kick and had tremendous speed. He once got dragged into a ruck when he was playing Pontypool. I spotted him, grinned and got him out: he was my mate!

Gerald Davies
Another man I was proud to play alongside. Another player justifiably known as a legend. Every fan knows about his pace and his sidestep. He was just quality. He represented a kind of elegance. Wales' greatest ever winger? For me, you'd have to be a brave person to argue against it.

130

Robert Paparemborde
The number one toughest opponent, I'd say. One of the strongest tightheads ever. He would screw you down to the deck if you let him. He was very, very good at turning in and trying to block the hooker. He knew all the tricks. He massacred everybody. They were all frightened of him. We had some very hard-fought battles on the pitch, but he invited me to his wedding!

His countrymen **Armand Vaquerin** and **Alain Estève** warrant a definite mention too. Mean as hell. Controversial on the pitch and off. They teamed up with **Jean-Louis Azarete** and **Alain Paco** to intimidate you. Estève was hard as nails. We stood up to them, though. We didn't take it if they were messing about or collapsing a scrum to protect their own ball. A sad aside: Vaquerin later tragically killed himself in a game of Russian Roulette.

Mike Gibson
The Ireland centre was pure class: versatile, skilful, an opponent you could watch and appreciate. He went on five Lions tours and, like me, played International rugby until he was in his late thirties.

I would like to mention a few players from Pontypool, because while there's always been a lot of talk of the Pontypool Front Row, there was also a very good back row. **Mike Harrington**, No. 8, and **Brian Gregory**, back-row forward, were very, very good club players. Neither ever got capped. Harrington was absolutely class at picking up the ball from the base of the scrum when we were going forward.

Got to mention Cob too – **Terry Cobner**. A great ally to Pross and the Pontypool Front Row. He completely took on Pross' philosophy and helped deliver it on the pitch. Both he and my old mate **Bobby Windsor** were great at directing things on the pitch. They were like shop stewards, one of the boys once said. And, of course, **Graham Price**. In the years we played together, Bobby, Graham and me became as one. A team within a team. That's unusual. The three of us didn't socialise together much off the pitch but when we played rugby, we were like blood-brothers – like we knew what each other was thinking.

And my other old mate **Mike 'Spike' Watkins**. Never far from trouble – on and off the pitch – Mike was one of the game's great 'jack-the-lads', but he was always brilliant for me, and a respected captain. He also captained the Wales 'B' side in a victory in France. Spike lives out in Thailand now, but he's still a good friend.

Rugby career statistics

PLAYING

Clubs: Whitehead's; Newport Saracens (*c.*70 appearances); Cross Keys (*c.*100 appearances); Pontypool (210 appearances, 12 tries)

Other appearances include: Gwent; Monmouthshire; Cwmbran Charitables; the TA; Crawshay's Welsh RFC; Major Stanley XV (invitational squad to play Oxford University); Carwyn James' International XV; Barbarians; Newport RFC (I stepped in a few times to cover injuries when I was coach); East Wales

For the 1977 British & Irish Lions I played two games in New Zealand and one against Fiji.

I played a number of uncapped games for Wales and 19 full Tests. Of the 19 I appeared in, we won 14 and lost 5. I scored four Test points.

My Test career looked like this:

> **Key:**
> FN = Five Nations match
> W = won
> L = lost
> The Wales score is shown first each time

1975

v France (Paris)	W25-10	(FN)
v England (Cardiff)	W20-4	(FN)
v Scotland (Murrayfield)	L10-12	(FN)
v Ireland (Cardiff)	W32-4	(FN)

➜**WALES WIN 1975 FIVE NATIONS**

v Australia (Cardiff)	W28-3

1976

v England (Twickenham)	W21-9	(FN)
v Scotland (Cardiff)	W28-6	(FN)
v Ireland (Dublin)	W34-9	(FN)
v France (Cardiff)	W19-13	(FN)

➜**WALES WIN 1976 FIVE NATIONS WITH GRAND SLAM AND TRIPLE CROWN**

1977

CHARLIE DID NOT PLAY

1978

v England (Twickenham)	W9-6	(FN)
v Scotland (Cardiff)	W22-14	(FN)
v Ireland (Dublin)	W20-16	(FN)
v France (Cardiff)	W16-7	(FN)

➜**WALES WIN 1978 FIVE NATIONS WITH GRAND SLAM AND TRIPLE CROWN**

v Australia (Brisbane)	L8-18
v Australia (Sydney)	L17-19
v New Zealand (Cardiff)	L12-13

1979

v Scotland (Murrayfield)	W19-13	(FN)
v Ireland (Cardiff)	W24-21	(FN)
v France (Paris)	L13-14	(FN)

→**WALES WIN 1979 FIVE NATIONS
WITH TRIPLE CROWN**

COACHING

The SAS; Newport Saracens; Newport RFC; Team GB (Maccabiah Games); Cardiff RFC; Wales Women; Caerphilly; St Peter's

Tributes to Charlie

CHARLIE FAULKNER DIED on 9 February 2023 at his home in Newport after a short illness. He was 81. The previous weekend he had sat with friends and family to watch Ireland win convincingly in Cardiff in the opening match of what was to be a difficult Six Nations for his beloved Wales.

There was a minute's silence at many grounds in the days following his death and there was a tribute to Charlie on the big screen at the Principality Stadium when Wales next took the field there.

Pontypool RFC were among the first to pay tribute, saying on Twitter:

> Charlie was a much-loved character and a massive part of the history of Pontypool RFC. He will be greatly missed by all who knew him. Everyone at Pontypool RFC send their deepest sympathy and sincere condolences to Charlie's family at this very difficult time.

Later the **Chairman, Pete Jeffreys**, added: "Legend is often an overused word in sport, but not in Charlie's case. He was a true legend of our game."

The WRU described Charlie as a "legendary loosehead prop", while a statement from **Cardiff President, Peter Thomas**, who has also since sadly died, stated:

> Charlie was a special person and an inspirational character whose company you would always want to have.
> Charlie was an outstanding coach who knew the importance of performing at the highest level, having been

part of the famous Pontypool, Wales and British and Irish Lions' front row. There is no doubt that Charlie will be sadly missed but never forgotten.

Jonathan Davies, a player at Cardiff under Charlie, said:

He was one of those characters that you had to be around, you needed in the changing room, always made everyone laugh, always made everyone welcome. He was just a funny guy; a great guy to have in your squad.

Crawshay's Rugby Club called Charlie a "genuine character of the game and a very tough competitor".

Many more tributes have been collected for this book:

Charlie was a great inspiration for training and fitness. He had a routine run and reps around Tredegar Park on Sunday morning. We would meet at 11:00. Charlie was coaching Newport and I had finished my rugby days and he encouraged a few people to join in and keep themselves fit. Money couldn't buy the kind of workout you got with Charlie.

When he coached, nobody could say he had not done the hard road! He put a lot back into rugby, as many a club and player will tell you.

When my wife Jacqui and I spent time with Charlie and Jill at their apartment in Spain, we would do a three-mile walk around Frigiliana every morning. This was a circuit with plenty of ups and downs to test you and, just before the home run to the apartment, we stopped in a small park and did the usual reps – never shortening them, however tired we were.

Then to finish it was a good slog uphill to the apartment, both feeling the pace now but pushing ourselves. I said to Charlie as we were getting nearer the finish, "You alright?" He spat out, "I'm alright, why?"

"Good," I said.

We were really feeling it now, pushing on to the finish at his front door. It was a hard one for us both, by any standard.

As we were about to step through the door, I said to him, "Let's do it again!" – I was joking. He turned around and off he went, with me behind, telling him I was only having a laugh!

This was the extra bit of attitude and discipline that he had – the extra that makes the difference in any person aspiring to get to the top.

**John Blackborow: Newbridge,
Newport United, Newport Saracens**

Tony Faulkner (Charlie) was simply one of the great characters of Welsh and British rugby. He was a gentle, likeable soul with a warm and ready smile for everyone. Despite not being a big man compared to some of the players of today, he perfected the dark arts of scrummaging with his own special technique and commanded respect from all his peers. Over his long and illustrious career, Charlie never lost his enthusiasm for the game he loved. I used to tease him I bought a Charlie Faulkner centenary tie in a charity shop in Cardiff. He was a dear friend, a proud member of the Pontypool Front Row – known affectionately as the Viet Gwent – and he will be sadly missed by all those who had the privilege of knowing him. Up and under here we go.

Max Boyce

I knew Charlie for sixty years. He was a great fella, and a man who took his rugby very seriously. He wasn't a natural, so he had to work hard to get where he did. The success he had at Pontypool and the caps he had for Wales were a tribute to the effort he put in. He got to the top through hard work and dedication to the game. He was a great friend who'd do anything for you. He was a character and there were so many stories about him over the years – they were all true!

**John 'Paddy' Burke: Whitehead's,
Cross Keys and Newport Saracens**

I remember when I was in my first year at Cardiff RFC, I was invited to play for Major Stanley's XV against Oxford University. I was just a young kid, really, and I'm not sure how I got picked, because the side included legends like Andy Irvine, Andy Ripley, Roger Uttley and the Pontypool Front Row. I travelled from Cardiff on my student rail ticket because I didn't know any of the Welsh boys then. We played the game and afterwards had a drink in the pavilion at Iffley Road. Tony came up to me and said, "How are you getting home, son?" and I said, "Oh, I'm on the train." He said, "No, come with us." And I remember being in the car with Tony, Pricey and Terry Cobner and I was completely starstruck! I was only about 18 or 19 and thinking, 'If my friends could see me now'!

For me, Tony – I always called him Tony; out of respect, I suppose – was old school in the very best way. He always prided himself on being smart and being polite. He was a gentleman.

When he coached at Cardiff, he worked closely with Terry Holmes and Alec Evans, and the players just loved him: not just for his personality, but for his knowledge and his experience. He was a technician of the scrum, from his head right down to his toes.

He and the Pontypool Front Row had a huge impact on Welsh rugby. They were known around the world. They all had different personalities, different skills, but when they worked together, they were simply *formidable*. That's why they are a legend which endures.

But my lasting memory of him will be his infectious laugh and beaming smile. Whether it was him who'd said something funny or someone else, his laugh and smile would light up the room.

Gareth Davies: Cardiff, Wales and the British & Irish Lions, and former Chairman of the WRU

Charlie played in one of the hardest positions in rugby football – a position which was competitive, punishing, aggressive, awkward and often violent, and he was one of the very toughest of prop forwards. But he was also one of the nicest of people. After a game, no matter what had happened, he was genial and smiling, always in good form; he was a lovely man.

Rugby-wise, he was always looking to learn and improve. Because I was on the wing, he knew I could get a particular view of the game and, after the final whistle, he would come up to me for a chat. He wanted to know how I'd viewed play, how things looked with the scrum and with his own play.

Because he was so well-qualified in judo, he knew a lot about balance, technique and position of the feet, and he took those judo skills and adapted them to the scrum.

And I remember to this day the very first time he said to me, "I may go up in the scrum, I may go down, but I never go back." Perhaps with an expletive in "I never go back"!

He, Graham and Bobby – the Pontypool Front Row – were a unit and you cannot isolate any one of them from the three. Together they made a substantial difference to the way people saw the Welsh team, because at one stage Wales was viewed as 'easy meat', without any toughness in the scrum. But the Pontypool Front Row shattered that view. When they came along, every team knew they were in for a tough afternoon. They were brilliant and such an important part of the Welsh team.

Gerald Davies: Cardiff, Wales and the British & Irish Lions, current President of the WRU

Charlie and Jill have been family friends for more than 50 years. My father Jim Davies played for Llanelli in the 1930s and, as he developed his businesses around Cardiff, he really wanted to help top amateur rugby players. Bleddyn Williams worked for him in the 1950s and in the 1970s he arranged for his friend Sir Kenneth Shelby of the Bath and Portland Group to look after Tom David and Steve Fenwick.

Dad took a shine to Charlie and they regularly went out to dinner, often to Rabaiotti's on the Esplanade in Penarth. One night they came back to our home and Dad showed him my rugby museum that I was gradually building up. He remembered, and sent me a poster autographed by all three of the Pontypool Front Row.

Then, a couple of years ago, the British & Irish Lions presented all former Lions with caps. Charlie was number 549 and he very kindly gave it to me. I was very honoured.

Philip Davies: family friend

The first time I came across Tony was when I played for Cardiff against Pontypool on a Wednesday night. It was a really difficult place to go and not a fixture that many of our players relished.

Then we played together for Wales, and it was good to have Tony on our side. The Pontypool Front Row were a class act and world-renowned, and they'd won everything in the game, so they were a great inspiration to the younger players.

When we were coaching together at Cardiff, he was such fun to be around. When we had a bad loss, even though a loss hurt him, he would pick us up again. He was very demanding on the front row: often training would end but the front five would be kept out there for 30 or 40 minutes longer.

Tony had such a passion for the game. He appreciated what rugby had given him. We both came from working-class families and realised that the game had been very good to us, allowing us to travel and represent our country.

Was he the best prop ever? Probably not. Was he the greatest coach ever? Probably not. But if you were looking for the complete package of player, coach, character and the man, then he'd be up there with the all-time greats.

Everyone loved Tony and he made friends everywhere he went. In 1995 we went on a trip to the Rugby World Cup in South Africa, and we were invited to go out on a boat to help change the shark nets. The team on the boat were all from the Zulu tribe. Tony was working hard with them, singing their songs, and pulling in the nets. By the end of the journey, he was lying in among them, asleep on the deck.

When the World Cup final came around, Tony decided there was something else he had to do. He loved the military and history, so instead of going to the final with us, Tony visited Rorke's Drift and watched the match on television.

He was such a character. He was humble, a gentleman, and great company both on and off the training pitch. I miss him very much.

It was such a pleasure and honour to coach with him. Working with him was some of the best times I've had in rugby.

There'll never be another Tony Faulkner. Rugby is a poorer sport without him.

**Terry Holmes: Cardiff, Wales
and British & Irish Lions**

He was an absolute gentleman, a great guy. His knowledge of the game was immense. He was very generous and enjoyed everything about rugby and being in players' company. I played rugby for a long time, under some great coaches, but he was the best forwards coach I've ever come across. He should have coached Wales. He'd have gone along and helped them if they'd asked. I hold Charlie in very high esteem. He was like a father figure to me and a lot of younger players.

**Dai Lubin: Glamorgan Wanderers,
Team GB (Maccabiah Games)**

The Pontypool Front Row always had our own game-within-a-game that we had to win. Pushing the opposition back at scrum time, to win a penalty, meant as much to us as any of those memorable tries you've seen the Welsh backs score.

People used to believe the Pontypool Front Row was indestructible. Certainly, we had our own little motto at scrum time, thought up by Charlie: "We may go up, we may go down, but we never go back."

And while there are plenty of stories and jokes about Charlie, the one thing he never did was make errors on the pitch. As we were ordered to do lap upon lap around the pitch in training, we were told rugby is about 80% fitness, 10% ability and 10% luck. But you make your own luck – and Charlie certainly made his.

The three of us were together through thick and thin. Our jerseys – 1, 2, 3 – were there next to one another when we entered the dressing room. If we went for a walk, say to the cinema in Cardiff city centre, we'd naturally default to Charlie one side, me the other, and Bobby in the middle.

It was an incredible period, on and off the pitch. The memories will never leave.

Charlie was in a class of his own at loosehead prop.

**Graham Price: Pontypool, Wales
and the British & Irish Lions**

He leaves an immense legacy as a great rugby character. He was one of the greatest of all Welsh rugby characters. Very popular with fellow forwards. Even if pacifist full backs like me weren't quite on the same wavelength! He was a forwards man to his boots.

The fact that he came from the Pontypool Front Row, which became the first ever club front row to play for the Lions – it puts him up there with the legends of Welsh rugby.

He made scrummaging into a science. When he talked about forward play, his whole countenance would change. He was passionate about the scrum. Obsessed with it. It was his life's work really, you know.

As well as that, you've got the mythology about his age, which added to the legend. I think he was always worried they'd say he was too old, and that drove him on.

If you listen to Brynmor Williams, Steve Fenwick and Gareth Edwards – all the greats – they've all got a Charlie story.

Phil Steele: Newport RFC, broadcaster

143

Anthony George Faulkner... He had to become Charlie: Ray Prosser at Pontypool only recognized nicknames! Would he have been capped today? Probably not – too old to start at almost 34. But like the great Tommy Smith at Liverpool, he was not born, he was quarried! He was one of the stone masons who provided the foundations of the 1975 success story and beyond... The Pontypool Front Row: where would we have been without them?

Bob Symonds: broadcaster

As such a passionate Welshman, Charlie was determined to help us improve. A genuine legend of the game, a nice guy and a gentleman. We were quite simply in awe of him, hanging on his every word. Although I do remember when my fellow second row Sam James left him speechless. He was showing us scrummaging techniques when she said, "Charlie, pull up your tracksuit bottoms. I'm not binding behind that bare crack!"

When representing our country, we were paying for our own match kit, transport and training camps and counted on people like Charlie to give us their time.

A few years later, while in Edinburgh watching the Wales men's and women's Six Nations, I bumped into him on Princes Street. He greeted me like an old friend and we had a proper old laugh.

Lisa Walsh (née Jones): Cardiff High School Old Boys (now Cardiff Quins RFC) and Wales

One of the things I have never forgotten from my first days of hosting rugby coverage for BBC Wales back in 1987 was the introductory monologue given by the formidable executive producer, Dewi Griffiths. "Television," he said, "is entertainment, and we have to tell the story in an entertaining way, otherwise we'll all be out of business!"

Well, in Welsh rugby we'd had plenty of entertainers; players who only needed one name or a set of initials. Barry,

Gareth, Phil, JJ, JPR, Gerald, Merv... And then, of course, we had the Pontypool Front Row – or the 'Viet Gwent', as myth would have us believe.

The reality of playing in that front row is an experience only Charlie Faulkner, Bobby Windsor and Graham Price could begin to describe. But did they let anyone outside of their cantonment know what tricks they got up to? Of course they didn't. It was their private parish.

Charlie gripped the secret most tightly, by speaking the least of the three of them. He just did what he did best: scrummaged the hell out of his opposite number to leave him bent and twisted. And our TV pictures took these angels of aggro, in their vivid red jerseys, and helped elevate them from sporting heroes of a special age to timeless legends of Welsh folklore.

Entertainment? You're damn right it was. Realistic? Too bloody true it was.

Charlie Faulkner? His myth will forever be.

Alan Wilkins: broadcaster

Tony 'Charlie' Faulkner was a massive influence on my playing and coaching career. He wanted to get the best out of every single player. It was never about him, it was always about the players, the team. If he saw something in a player, he'd give them his time. He had a heart of gold and a natural ability to make players want to go that extra mile for him. He'd find things to help them in their play, a little bit of advice. Players idolised him. That is why, in my opinion, he was greatly underrated as a coach. There are lots of funny stories about Tony but he always knew he was being funny and people don't always realise that. He was a very bright man. I will never forget him. My admiration and gratitude will never fade.

Alun Williams: Newport RFC,
Cardiff Met RFC coach

Although not playing in one of the fashionable positions, Charlie was vital to the success of the Seventies and was a legend in his own right. The obvious superstars, of course, were Gareth, Benny, JPR, JJ and Gerald, but they will all say their success was built on the shoulders of the forward pack, where players like the great Charlie Faulkner did his job exceptionally well.

The quality of work undertaken by Charlie and front-row colleagues in the close-quarter stuff was incredible and, of course, enabled the hugely skilful and exciting back line to shine.

His presence and humour in the dressing room also played a huge part in things. He would have us laughing a lot and it regularly punctured the pre-match tension and relaxed the mood in the camp. His emphasis on the physicality of the battle was both serious and funny. No-one was as determined as him to overcome his opponent.

His psychological build-up for the huge physical confrontation ahead was also very funny and very focussed, and the throw-away remarks regarding his tighthead opponent, like, "He'll have to f***ing have it" or "He's got it f***ing coming to him" or "I will dominate him like his f***ing wife does" or often, to coach John Dawes just before we left the dressing room, "I might go up, John, and I might go down, but I won't go f***ing back", were classics before every game.

He was a much-loved, respected and admired character. His name will forever be synonymous with technical expertise and second-to-none commitment in the front row.

One of the memories that stands out in my mind is of Charlie, after dismantling the huge and great French prop Paparemborde, sitting by himself in the Angel Hotel for after-match dinner drinks. He was there in his smart Welsh blazer with all the buttons done up, sitting and staring forward, nodding and smiling quietly to himself. He was clearly approving his own outstanding performance and reflecting on his important contribution. I asked him if he wanted a drink and he said, "Make it a large whisky, my friend, and a very large cigar. Job well done, job well f***ing done, see, Bryn?"

Indeed, his job was always well done. A great guy. And, unfortunately, they don't make them like Charlie anymore.

Brynmor Williams: Cardiff, Newport RFC, Swansea, Wales and the British & Irish Lions

I first met Charlie when I started at the steelworks and he pinched my sandwiches. We worked alongside each other among the white-hot metal. It was physical work and it was good for us. And as we got more serious with the rugby, we'd find further ways to get fit and stronger. We'd make weights with big metal balls hanging from straps, which we'd use to strengthen our necks. Other times, we'd take our kit into work and get the boys to cover for us in the mill. We'd jump over the wall and run down to Tredegar Park, where we'd do a training circuit, up over the golf links, run back and jump back over the fence. The great Ray Prosser would say the game is 90% fitness and we lived by that. Skill wasn't enough. We wanted to make sure the other side would never be fitter than us. In a game, Charlie and I never wanted the referee to blow the whistle: we were enjoying ourselves too much!

We started the hard way, in junior rugby, against experienced front-row men who'd tie you up in knots. But we survived and we learned. And we did it together. Playing for the Sarries was great, but then we were proud as punch to play first class at Cross Keys. Great bunch, great club. Then Pontypool. Charlie's move there was fantastic for Charlie and fantastic for Pontypool too. And when we got back together and we played for Wales, we'd gone from the bottom to the top.

Charlie was put under a hell of a lot of pressure by the press. In those days, if you were 30, you were finished. Even when I joined Wales, one of the players told me to knock two years off my age. Well, I was a lot younger than Charlie. So he kept extra fit. He gave all that he had, and he had more than everyone else because he trained so hard.

Charlie was a character. You've heard the stories. They're all true. I mean, you've read about the 'grey' cat [see pages 42–43]. That's all true. Typical! We had our story all sorted, but the only thing we didn't discuss in advance was the colour of the cat!

More than this, Charlie was the right man to have alongside you. There was a lot of stuff going on in the scrum in those days, a lot of stuff. The French games, well, there were boots coming through the scrum without mercy. I'd see them check out where the ref was and then the boot would come through. It was no place to be on your own. I'd give Charlie the word, the signal, say I was in trouble, and he'd back me up.

I'd go fighting tigers with Charlie. A top man in judo, a top man in rugby. I played with some greats: Fran Cotton, 'Mighty Mouse' McLauchlan, Mike Burton. Great, great players. But if I had to have anyone by me, it would have to be Charlie. He would give it all for you – every single time.

When Charlie died, I lost my Number One. My Number One. And I mean that in every way – playing-wise and as a friend off the field.

Bobby Windsor: Whitehead's, Cross Keys, Newport Saracens, Pontypool, Wales and British & Irish Lions

And finally…

Some wonderful 'Faulknerisms':

"We'll be up to our mud in ankles."

To Rhys Morgan, who was propping against Iain Milne: "Don't forget, now, if this Iain Milne takes the scrum down, give him a good fucking booting, because it's dangerous to drop the scrum, Rhys!"

Charlie at the hotel breakfast on the morning after arriving in New Zealand on the 1977 Lions tour: "What, 60 million sheep and no bacon?"

A Faulknerism via Graham Price:

> We had everything paid for on tour – flights, accommodation, meals – except phone calls. Back then, of course, there were no mobiles and you couldn't just direct dial, you had to go through the switchboard.
>
> Charlie wanted to ring home from Japan in 1975 but didn't want to pay for it. In the team room, with a mountain of beer around us and feeling rather jolly, he spotted a phone on the wall.
>
> "Tell them you're Mervyn Davies," we told Charlie. As captain, Merv had special privileges. His phone calls to Wales were free. He was the only one.
>
> Over Charlie wandered, picked up the receiver. "Hello, my name is Mervyn Davies, I'm the Wales captain and I'd like to make an international call to Newport, south Wales," we

heard Charlie say, giving the switchboard the appropriate number.

"Thank-you, we're quite busy this evening but I will phone you back in 20 minutes when I make the connection," came the reply.

We carried on drinking for half an hour or so, and, when the phone rang, we told Charlie to answer.

"Good evening, I have an international call here for a Mr Mervyn Davies. Is he there please?" asked the switchboard operator.

Charlie looked around the room, and suddenly asked the rest of us, "Anybody seen Merv?"

"No," came the reply.

"Sorry love, he's not here," said Charlie, promptly hanging up the phone.

Priceless!

As Phil Steele says, "That's one of the reasons why people loved him, because he said these things. Maybe he knew he was being funny. Maybe he was double-bluffing the lot of us."

Author's note

COMPLETING THIS BOOK after Tony's death was obviously a challenge, but his family was determined that his story be told. My first thanks go to them for their support.

I would also like to thank my former *South Wales Echo* colleague Steve Jones and my good friend Len Mullins for taking the time to read the manuscript with such care and attention; John Blackborow for all his help and for answering my incessant questions; John 'Paddy' Burke, Dai Lubin, Jem Spence, Phil Steele, George Thomas and Noel Williams for all their help with background information; and huge thanks to our editor at Y Lolfa, Carolyn Hodges, for all her work to help bring this book to fruition. Special thanks to Graham Price, Paul Abbandonato and Wales Online/Media Wales for permission to quote in the book from Graham's tribute to Tony.

Everyone contacted to pay tribute to Tony was eager to help and generous with their time, and it was a pleasure to speak to so many friends of Tony's and legends of Welsh rugby. Speaking of legends, huge thanks go to Sir Gareth Edwards, who contributed his foreword right at the outset of the project and gave the book its momentum.

On a final personal note, I'd like to dedicate this book to my dear friend, Will Davies, who supported me at the start but sadly died before the book was completed. He was an enthusiastic collector and teller of stories, and would have adored this book, from Gareth's opening words to the humour of the final Faulknerisms. Like Tony, you are much missed, Will.

Greg Lewis
September 2023

151

Also from Y Lolfa:

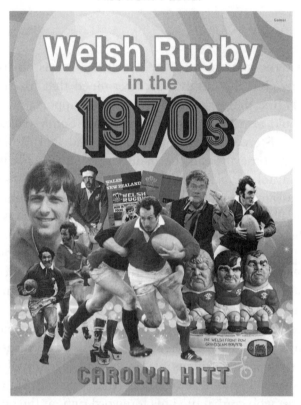

£14.99

Fun retro-style hardback celebrating the
Golden Era of Welsh Rugby

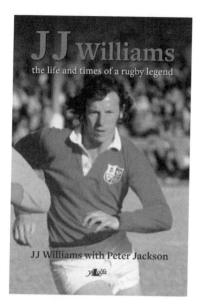

£14.99

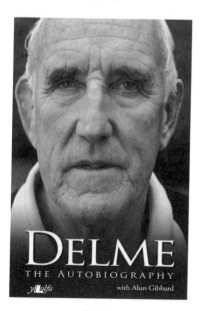

£9.95

Revealing autobiographies of two icons of 1970s Welsh rugby

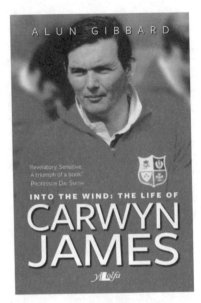

£14.99

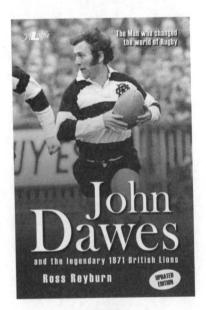

£9.99

Acclaimed biographies of two of the
greatest coaches to grace the Welsh game

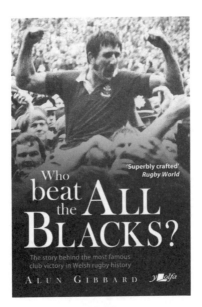

£9.99

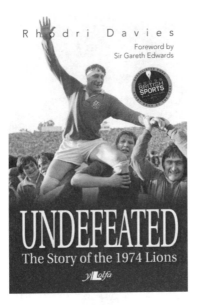

£9.95

The full stories of the All Blacks' 1970s
defeats at the hands of Llanelli and the Lions

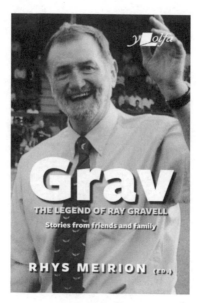

£7.99

£7.95

More legends of the Welsh game

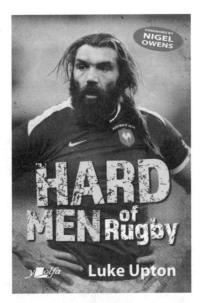

£9.99

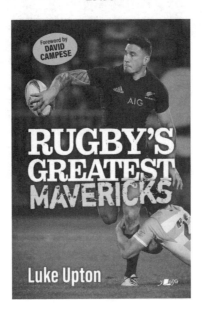

£12.99

The fascinating stories of some of the most
iconic players ever, from all around the rugby world

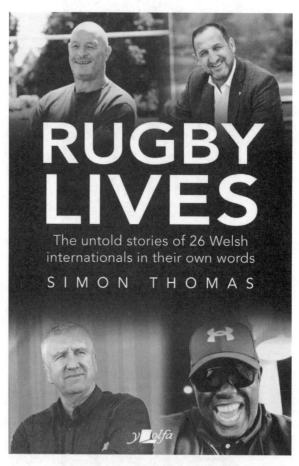

RUGBY
LIVES

The untold stories of 26 Welsh
internationals in their own words

S I M O N   T H O M A S

y Lolfa

£12.99

In-depth interviews looking back on the
careers of 26 of Welsh rugby's finest players

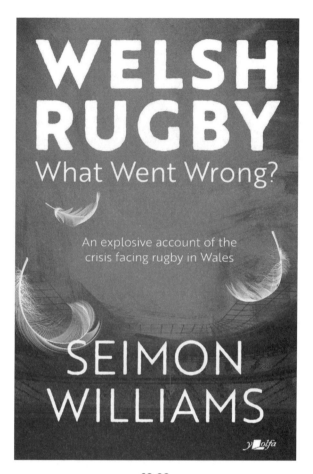

WELSH RUGBY
What Went Wrong?

An explosive account of the
crisis facing rugby in Wales

SEIMON
WILLIAMS

y Lolfa

£9.99

Analysis of the key events which have
brought Welsh rugby to its present crisis

Ask for a print quote!
www.ylolfa.com